DATE DUE

8

MOTHER JONES

MOTHER JONES

Fierce Fighter for Workers' Rights

Judith Pinkerton Josephson

Lerner Publications Company • Minneapolis

For my daughters, Kirsten and Erika, with love

For their detailed critiques of the manuscript, thanks to Edith Fine, Karen Coombs, Pat Brunini, Mary Pinkerton, Catherine Koemptgen, and my wonderful Encinitas writers' group. My research was made possible by the Malcolm Love Library at San Diego State University, the Denver Public Library (Western History Department), the Chicago Historical Society, Catholic University of America, the Carlsbad Public Library, the Labor Hall of Fame, and the extensive compilation of Mother Jones's speeches, letters, and life events found in works by Edward M. Steel, Philip S. Foner, Dale Fetherling, and Ronnie Gilbert. For permissions granted, thanks to the Charles H. Kerr Co., Chicago, Illinois.

My gratitude to my editor, Sara Saetre, for helping me shape and sharpen my words, as well as corral the astounding number of details in Mother Jones's life into book form. Thanks to my husband, Ron, and to my daughters for their support and encouragement.

Library of Congress Cataloging-in-Publication Data

Josephson, Judith Pinkerton
    Mother Jones: fierce fighter for workers' rights/Judith Pinkerton Josephson.
        p. cm.
    Includes bibliographical references and index.
    Summary: A biography of Mary Harris Jones, the union organizer who worked tirelessly for the rights of workers.
    ISBN 0-8225-4924-7 (alk. paper)
    1. Jones, Mother, 1843?–1930—Juvenile literature. 2. Women labor leaders—United States—Biography—Juvenile literature. 3. Women in the labor movement—United States—Biography—Juvenile literature. 4. Children—Employment—United States—History—Juvenile literature. 5. Labor movement—United States—Juvenile literature. [1. Jones, Mother, 1843?–1930. 2. Labor leaders. 3. Women—Biography.] I. Title.
HD8073.J6J67 1997
331.88'092—dc20
    [B]   96-11802

Manufactured in the United States of America
1 2 3 4 5 6 – JR – 02 01 00 99 98 97

Contents

Preface 7

1 *Jail Songs* 9

2 *"Born in Revolution"* 15

3 *Out of the Ashes, a New Purpose* 23

4 *Shutdown on the Railroad* 35

5 *"Suffer the Little Children"* 43

6 *"Boys, Listen to Me"* 53

7 *An Army of Women with Mops
   and Brooms* 59

8 *Trouble in West Virginia* 71

9 *The March of the Mill Children* 83

10 *Mad Dogs in Colorado* 95

11 *The Most Dangerous Woman
    in America* 105

12 *"Women Are Fighters"* 121

13 *"An Old War Horse Wearing Down"* . . 129

Sources 138

Bibliography 141

Index 142

Preface

Much of what we know about Mother Jones comes from her many letters and speeches and from her autobiography. In her writings, she often misspelled or left out words. She was careless about punctuation marks and capital letters. She didn't pay much attention to keeping dates, locations, and other facts straight. Sometimes she gave slightly different accounts of the same events.

Because of this, no one is certain of some facts about Mother Jones. For example, historians don't know for sure when she was born, when she came to the United States, how many children she had, and where she lived during some years. For this book, I sifted through Mother Jones's own words, as well as through newspaper articles and books written about her, to come as close to the facts as possible.

As a union organizer in the days before labor unions were well established, Mother Jones had to work hard to gain attention for workers' causes. Sometimes she used strong language in her speeches. She said swearing was how she woke people up and got action. She also said swearing was how working people prayed, especially when they wanted a quick answer. In this book, I've quoted Mother Jones's words, complete with her own misspellings, her own hasty punctuation—and the sometimes peppery words she herself chose.

Mother Jones's gentle looks masked a fighting spirit as fierce as that of a mother lion.

ONE

Jail Songs
1910

Angry women milled about the small jail cell in Greensburg, Pennsylvania. The crowded room was noisy, filled with mothers holding crying babies. Mother Jones, a short, elderly woman, visited with the prisoners, offering comforting words to them and patting their babies.

Dressed neatly in a bonnet trimmed with pansies and a long, black dress, Mother Jones seemed strangely out of place in a jail cell. Her piercing blue eyes looked out from behind wire-rimmed glasses. Wispy, snow-white hair framed her soft, wrinkled face. At seventy-seven, she looked like a kindly grandmother. But the firm set of her mouth showed grit and determination.

This was the same woman who had trudged up mountains and waded across creeks to remote mining camps. There she had urged miners to join a labor union. Railroads, coal mines, cotton mills, and other industries in the United States were booming. But few in the working class shared the wealth and power enjoyed by company owners (or "bosses," as Mother Jones thought of them).

To fight for better wages and working conditions, workers in many industries had banded together into labor unions. When talks broke down between a labor union and company bosses, workers sometimes left their jobs and went on strike.

The company then had several choices. It could shut down; it could give in to strikers' demands; or it could bring in other workers to replace the strikers. The new workers—called "strikebreakers" by company bosses and "scabs" by strikers—accepted the companies' wages and working conditions without complaint. A company could conduct business as usual.

The practice of hiring scabs made strikers mad. Often a company hired private detectives or even guards to protect scabs from strikers. If one or both sides grew violent, a governor—or even the United States president—called in soldiers. Many strikes turned into small wars, with people on both sides being hurt or killed.

But violence didn't scare Mother Jones. During countless labor battles, she faced company guards toting machine guns. Swearing, she dared them to shoot her, "an old woman." Her strike activities pitted her solidly against big business and the law. A lawyer once called her "the most dangerous woman in the country today."

A few days before Mother Jones visited the women jailed in Greensburg, the women had gathered at the entrance to the coal mine where their husbands worked. The men were on strike, and the wives had hooted and shouted at the company's scabs. Police had arrested the women for disturbing the peace.

At the women's court hearing, their babies fussed loudly. The judge complained: Why hadn't the mothers left their children at home? Mother Jones whispered to one of the women to tell the judge that "miners' wives didn't keep nurse girls.... God gave the children to their mothers and He held them responsible for their care."

When the woman told the judge this, he scowled angrily. He sentenced the prisoners to thirty days in jail or a fine of thirty dollars. Since thirty dollars was more than their husbands earned in a month, the women went to jail. The bosses of the coal mine had gotten their way. Company bosses often used their wealth and power to influence judges. They weren't about to let striking miners and their noisy wives shut down their mines.

Like the women jailed in Greensburg, these wives of Pennsylvania miners marched to support a 1910 strike.

Mother Jones didn't have wealth and power. She did have the mothers and their babies, and she had a plan. When she visited the women's jail cell, she told them, "You sing the whole night long. . . . Sleep all day and sing all night and don't stop for anyone. Say you're singing to the babies." Then Mother Jones rattled on the bars for the sheriff to open the door. Walking briskly, she left the jail.

That night, the miners' wives sang every song they knew—sometimes several at once—as loudly as they could. Their babies cried all night long. People in nearby houses could hear the racket coming from the windows of the jail.

Soon complaints flooded the sheriff's office. No one could sleep. When Mother Jones heard that tired neighbors had said that the women "howled like cats," she snapped, "That's no way to speak of women who are singing patriotic songs and lullabies to their little ones!" Unimpressed, the sheriff ordered her to stop the women.

"I can't stop them," she told him, "You telephone to the judge to order them loose." The judge wouldn't, and the women continued. So did the complaints. Finally, after five straight nights of the noise, the judge set the prisoners free.

"He was a narrow-minded, irritable, savage-looking old animal," Mother Jones said about the judge, "and [he] hated to [free them], but no one could muzzle those women!" Feisty Mother Jones had won.

The victory was one of many. For almost sixty years, Mother Jones fought tirelessly for the rights of workers. She crisscrossed the United States, going from one strike to another and moving thousands of people to action. When she spoke, her bonnet bobbed up and down. She shook her fist, prayed, and swore. Her listeners cheered loudly and sometimes cried. Even if they spoke another language (as

A notice alerted miners to walk out on their jobs.

was the case with many immigrant workers), they understood her anger and her impatience with injustice. She was on their side.

Mother Jones's toughness and bravery brought her to meetings with presidents, governors, senators, and other powerful people. She wasn't afraid of rich bosses, soldiers, or jails. When a college professor once praised her for being a "great humanitarian," she bristled, "Get it right. I'm not a humanitarian. I'm a hell raiser." During her long, restless life, she became one of the most forceful figures in the American labor movement.

Desperate Irish farm families were thrown out of their homes when they couldn't pay the rent.

TWO

"Born in Revolution"

1830–1865

"I was born in revolution," Mother Jones often said. Mary Harris Jones probably came into the world on May 1, 1830, in Cork, Ireland. The first child of Richard and Mary Harris, Mary lived with her family in a one-room thatched cottage. Built against a hill, the cottage stayed damp, even with a fire burning. Like other poor families in Ireland, the Harrises ate potatoes, oatmeal, and sometimes herring. When they had enough money, they kept a cow for milk. Meat was for rich people.

Mary's family farmed the rocky, weather-beaten fields around their cottage as tenant farmers for a British landlord. Tenant farmers received little money for themselves when crops were sold. Most of the profits went to the landlords. When crops failed, farmers had even less.

When British landlords raised rents for tenant farmers, many were thrown out of their homes because they couldn't pay. The poorest people starved. By the early 1830s, when Mary was a small child, homeless peasants began to burn and vandalize the property of their former landlords.

15

British soldiers were called in to stop them. The Irish formed secret groups to fight the soldiers. Mary once watched, horrified, as soldiers marched through the streets of her village with the heads of rebel peasants stuck on their bayonets.

The British government hanged Mary's grandfather for belonging to one of the secret groups. In 1835, soldiers broke into the Harris home looking for Mary's father. Richard Harris and some of his neighbors had secretly raided camps where some peasants were being held prisoner. As Mary clung to her mother's skirts, the soldiers tore the Harris's chimney apart, searching for Richard. But he had already fled the country, hidden on a fishing boat. His wife, five-year-old Mary, and Mary's younger brothers, Sean and Shamus, were on their own.

Before Mary's father had left, he had promised his family he would find them a home in America. He would work hard, save his money, and send for them when he could.

Mary's father was brawny, strong, and driven by hope. When he reached America, he found work on a construction crew building canals in New York. He became a United States citizen. He joined a railroad crew and was soon promoted to foreman. By 1838, he had enough money to send for his family.

Mary's family booked passage on a heavily loaded ship. Passengers rode packed together like cattle. They battled seasickness and stale air on the three-thousand-mile voyage from Cork to New York City. The rough trip across the Atlantic Ocean took seven weeks.

The Harrises settled in Toronto, Canada, where Mary's father continued to work for the railroad. Toronto was a bustling city of fifteen thousand where neat, wooden houses

Irish emigrants on a crowded ship waved good-bye.

lined the dirt roads. The Harrises had enough money to live comfortably. The family even owned two pigs—a luxury unheard of back in Ireland.

Mary's parents could barely read and write, but they wanted their children to be educated. So eight-year-old Mary and her brothers attended the new Toronto public school. To her parents' delight, Mary did well. When she finished elementary school, her father insisted she go on to high school. Mary's brothers left school to work for the railroad.

In high school, Mary became good at giving speeches and debating. A short young woman with bright blue eyes, she appeared almost frail up on stage. But when she spoke in her clear, strong voice tinged with an Irish brogue, her audience heard every word.

At home, Mary learned dressmaking from her mother. Mary could soon design clothes as well as sew them. To earn extra money, she made clothes for friends and neighbors.

Mary became the first in her family to graduate from high school. She then attended a college for training teachers. At that time, going to college was an unusual step for a young woman; most college students were male. Poor immigrant girls like Mary usually worked as maids or serving girls. But like her father, Mary had an adventurous spirit.

Mary left the college in 1847 at the age of seventeen, armed with two valuable skills: teaching and dressmaking. About this time, Mary's mother gave birth to another son, William. Over the next several years, Mary taught in Toronto and then in Maine in the United States. Because of her father's citizenship, Mary was also a United States citizen—something she was proud of.

In the fall of 1859, when Mary was twenty-nine, she taught at a convent school near Detroit, Michigan. Mary didn't enjoy enforcing the school's harsh rules. She wanted to teach in her own way. The following March, she left the school and collected her wages (low for the times) of $36.43 for six months of teaching. She moved to Chicago, Illinois, and set up shop as a dressmaker. "I preferred sewing to bossing little children," Mary said.

In 1860, Chicago was a growing trade center with almost two hundred thousand people. Even so, Mary found there wasn't enough dressmaking work for her to make a living.

Mary had heard that there were teaching jobs in Memphis, Tennessee. A city of thirty-three thousand people, Memphis was the sixth largest city in the South. As was common, female teachers were paid only a third as much as male teachers. In the fall of 1861, Mary accepted a job there anyway.

Mary had chosen a troubled time to move to Tennessee. For many years, the issue of slavery had bitterly divided the country. White plantation owners in Southern states depended on the cheap labor of their black slaves. Many Northerners wanted to see slavery outlawed. The state of Tennessee was on the border between the North and the South. Like the nation's citizens, the people of Tennessee were sharply divided over the issue of slavery.

In March 1861, Abraham Lincoln became president of the United States. In the weeks before and after he took office, eleven states angrily seceded, or withdrew, from the nation to form a separate government known as the Confederate States of America. The North became known as the Union. On April 12, 1861, Confederate troops fired on Fort Sumter in Charleston, South Carolina. The country was at war.

Soon after arriving in Memphis, Mary met George E. Jones, a tall, bespectacled young man. Strong and hardworking, George was a skilled iron molder. Though he had been raised in Tennessee, where slavery was common, he thought slavery was wrong. So did Mary. The city of Memphis seethed with war talk. Sometimes George appeared with a black eye or a bloody nose from arguing with pro-Confederate workers at the iron factory.

In December 1861—just a few months after they met—Mary and George married. The couple rented a small house

Life was often bleak in the "Pinchgut" district of Memphis.

in a Memphis slum called the "Pinchgut" district. The slum's residents were said to be so poor that their stomachs hurt from lack of food. People were crowded into shacks and run-down buildings. The drinking water ran brown and unclean. Human waste and other filth littered the streets.

Slowly, Mary began to understand the bleak lives of iron molders. A top iron molder at that time made twenty dollars a week. For this wage, George spent ten to twelve hours a day hunched over a bench in the half-light of a fiery forge, with clouds of smoke and steam swirling around him. The fire had to be hot enough to melt iron. Sometimes flames from the forge scorched a molder's skin and singed his hair. In the summertime, the heat inside the factory became almost unbearable.

George was a dedicated member of the Iron Molders International Union. Like other national unions that had begun to form in the 1850s, it was organized for workers in one trade. George's union wanted higher pay, better safety regulations, and blower systems for ventilation. Normally a serious, quiet man, George became lively and outspoken when he talked about his union. He told Mary his hopes for workers. He dreamed of a time when unions would provide funds for schooling, medical care, and housing.

Mary grew excited about George's ideas. Fighting for better working conditions made sense to her. She hated injustice and wanted to rebel against it. She began to feel that wives, too, had a stake in their husbands' unions. Freedom from oppression was important to every person.

Tennessee finally seceded and joined the Confederacy. With his skills as an iron molder, George continued to be a valuable worker. Iron molders crafted important wartime supplies. When the North captured the city of Memphis in 1862, the city's factories had to make weapons for the Union army. George and Mary didn't mind; their sympathies lay with the North.

The Civil War ended in 1865, four years after it had begun. The war had put an end to slavery. It had also destroyed countless homes and businesses in Memphis and other cities, killed 620,000 soldiers, and deeply scarred a nation.

Factories such as this one flourished after the Civil War, providing steady jobs for workers like George Jones.

THREE

Out of the Ashes, a New Purpose

1866–1877

After the war, life in Memphis was good for Mary and George Jones. Industries grew. People needed the tools and hardware made by iron molders to rebuild what had been destroyed by the fighting. Mary and George now had two young daughters, Catherine and Elizabeth. A son, Terence, was born soon after the war ended.

With the nation at peace, George threw all his energy into his union work. The iron workers elected him to a full-time post as a paid official of the Iron Molders International Union. He traveled around Tennessee and nearby states, urging workers to join the union.

Mary spent almost all her time caring for her young children. Her world centered on their happy chatter, warm hugs, and busy activities. But she listened eagerly when George returned from his travels and told her about his union work. She believed strongly in what he was trying to do. In 1866, another baby (whose name is not known) joined the Jones family. Mary's life was full and happy.

Then the summer of 1867 brought tragic change. An unusually rainy spring had swollen ponds and creeks around
Memphis. City streets flooded and became muddy swamps.
When summer came, blistering heat turned the stagnant
water into perfect breeding places for mosquitoes. The in-
sects swarmed over Memphis. Some of the mosquitoes carried the yellow fever virus.

Soon residents of Memphis began to come down with
this deadly disease. Victims ran a high fever and felt chills,
dizziness, and head and back pain. Their eyes and skin
turned yellow; then black blotches appeared on their skin.
Some lucky people got better after this stage of the illness.
Others grew worse, bleeding from their gums and vomiting a

Victims of yellow fever (left) *were buried quickly* (right).

black fluid. Finally they became delirious, dropped into a coma, and died. Their bodies gave off a horrible stench.

No one knew how to stop the epidemic. People thought "bad air" caused the disease. The citizens of Memphis burned strong-smelling sulfur torches outside to purify the air. They burned the sheets, towels, and clothing of those who had died. They scrubbed streets with disinfectant and carbolic acid. City officials banned public meetings to keep the virus from spreading.

But people probably knew these actions did little good. One health official admitted, "Yellow fever must run its course, and nothing that we know of can stop it."

The epidemic hit hard in the Pinchgut slum. The wild cries of the dying and the wails of their loved ones pierced the air. Death carts rumbled through the streets. Hooded, masked drivers called for families to bring out their dead. The corpses were buried quickly, without ceremony.

Mary and George watched helplessly as, one by one, their children fell ill. The children's rosy cheeks turned yellow. Their small bodies seemed to turn inside out with vomiting. First Catherine, Elizabeth, and Terence died. Then the baby. Near dawn one morning, Mary sobbed as she cradled her dead infant. Heartbroken, she washed her children's little bodies and got them ready for burial. But the horror wasn't over. Soon George came down with the fever. Within days, he too was dead.

Overcome with sorrow, Mary sat alone in her empty, silent house. "I sat alone through nights of grief," said Mary. "No one came to me. No one could. Other homes were as stricken as mine."

Death had carried away those Mary loved most. "All day long, all night long, I heard the grating of the wheels of the death cart," she said. Yet she did not catch the fever. She struggled to understand. Finally, she decided that she had been spared so she could help others.

A few days after George died, Mary volunteered to care for other yellow fever victims. She fed those too weak to eat without help and tended children whose parents were ill.

On October 15, 1867, members of the local chapter of George Jones's union held a special meeting to honor him. They draped their charter in dark mourning cloth for thirty days.

The yellow fever epidemic ended in December 1867. Almost 240 people had died—one out of every hundred people in Memphis. At thirty-seven, Mary was a childless widow. From then on, she spoke and wrote little about her terrible

When Mary moved back to Chicago, railroads and other industries were booming. But the lives of the rich contrasted sharply with those of the poor.

loss. Yet from this experience, an iron core began to form within her. She would survive. She would begin again.

Feeling that work would help ease her grief, Mary returned to Chicago and set up a dressmaking shop. The sign outside read "Mary Jones, Seamstress and Dressmaker." Mary lived in a small room at the back of the shop.

Since she had last been in Chicago, the city had expanded to more than 275,000 people, making it the largest city in the Midwest. Many residents had grown rich from the city's meat-packing houses, railroads, and other huge industries. Wealthy families lived in massive three-story mansions lining the shore of Lake Michigan.

Soon Mary's foot pumped the treadle of her sewing machine from morning until night. Her shop hummed with the

whir of her shuttle and the clickety-clack-clack of her needle. From colorful bolts of satin, silk, and fine linen, Mary created fashionable dresses and bonnets for her well-to-do customers. Sometimes she worked in the customers' beautiful homes.

Even while sewing for the rich, Mary often thought of the poor who lived in the slums on Chicago's West Side. Among them were many newly arrived immigrants. Hundreds of the working poor were children who labored in factories, shops, and packinghouses, often for less than fifty cents a week. The flimsy wooden shacks and rundown apartment buildings of the West Side looked far different from the elegant mansions on Lake Shore Drive.

Mary found the contrast between the lives of the poor and those of the rich painful. "Often while sewing for the lords and barons," she wrote, "I would look out of the plate glass windows and see the poor, shivering wretches, jobless and hungry, walking along the frozen lake front. . . . My employers seemed neither to notice nor to care."

The summer of 1871 was one of the hottest on record in Chicago. Only five inches of rain fell between May and October. Lawns shriveled and turned brown; wells ran dry. On Sunday night, October 8, 1871, a cow tipped over a lantern in a barn on the West Side belonging to Patrick O'Leary. Within seconds, the barn was ablaze.

Fed by a fierce wind, the fire spread quickly, gobbling up wooden buildings, fences, sidewalks, bridges, and pine-paved streets. Walls toppled. Superheated gusts of wind hurled sheets of fire forward almost half a mile at a time. The roar of the whirling masses of flame muffled the screams of frightened people. Residents flung possessions into wagons, wheelbarrows, and carriages and tried to flee the city. Streets

Mary's dressmaking shop was one of many buildings destroyed in the Great Chicago Fire.

became hopelessly clogged, slowing people's escape. Sparks and burning embers rained down on the panicked residents.

By dawn the next morning, the wind had driven the sea of fire northeast and across the Chicago River. The city's business district was ablaze. When the fire reached Mary's block, she ran from her shop carrying nothing but a sack of food.

The Great Chicago Fire raged for three days before weary firefighters and a pouring rain put out the blaze. It had destroyed much of the heart of the city. In all, eighteen thousand buildings had burned to the ground. The damage totaled almost two hundred million dollars. An estimated three hundred people had died.

Mary, along with ninety thousand other residents, was now homeless, her shop burned to rubble. At forty-one, Mary had again lost everything—everything except her sturdy spirit.

She spent the next few days camping with other homeless people in parks along the lake. She walked among the people, passing out food donated by residents of nearby towns. Later, she huddled with other fire victims in Old St. Mary's Catholic Church. It would have been easy for her to have given up. Instead, she organized soup kitchens, helped people find places to stay, and took care of the sick and the elderly.

An iron molder who had known Mary's husband told her about a labor group with branches all over the country. The Knights of Labor was the first labor group to try to organize all workers, regardless of their trades. The iron molder said the Knights wanted to improve workers' lives through education and better laws. The local branch met at a ramshackle building near St. Mary's.

Mary began attending meetings of the group. Powerful speakers talked about changing the way businesses were run. More control should be in the hands of the workers, they said. The speakers' words made Mary think about her late husband's strong union beliefs and about the Irish peasants who had died fighting the tyranny of the British. Mary liked the high ideals she saw and the sense of belonging she felt in the Knights of Labor. She began to work as a volunteer for the group.

Meanwhile, Chicago began to recover from the fire—the worst disaster in its history. The rebuilding began almost before the ashes grew cold. New residents continued to flood into the growing city. Within two years of the fire, bare land in the business district was worth more than it had been with buildings on it.

Even so, Mary, like other poor citizens, struggled. People needed to replace clothing lost in the fire, so she returned to dressmaking. She also spent more and more time volunteering for the Knights of Labor. Working as an organizer, she explained the group to workers and urged them to join. At that time, workers in many trades put in twelve to fourteen hours a day in dangerous jobs. Mary thought the Knights of Labor offered the best weapon with which to fight for better conditions.

Thirty labor unions already existed in the United States, most of them for workers in one trade or craft. (The iron molders union had been one of the first.) In all, the unions had three hundred thousand members. But the push to organize was just beginning. It wasn't easy. Some people distrusted labor groups like the Knights. Workers, afraid of losing their jobs, hesitated to join, in spite of the harsh lives they lived.

Now in her early forties, Mary had a distinct, motherly appearance. She drew her long, soft hair into a bun at the back of her head. Dressed neatly in clothes she had sewn herself, Mary always wore long, black dresses or skirts. She trimmed her dresses and shirtwaists, or blouses, with bits of flowers, flounces of lace, lavender vests, or shawls.

From the start of her work with the Knights of Labor, Mary stood out because she was a woman. Few women had joined the Knights. Fewer still were organizers. Mary was well educated and a good speaker. Her voice didn't rise when she made an important point, but dropped even lower. Poet Carl Sandburg once described her clear voice as "a singing voice." Whether striding about the stage in a rage or coaxing the audience into laughter, she knew how to tell a story. And she was persuasive. One observer said, "She could talk blood out of a stone."

A few years after the Great Chicago Fire, Mary traveled to San Francisco and briefly joined a labor fight. She also visited Europe to study working conditions there. More than likely, her friends in the labor movement pooled their money with hers to help pay for her travels.

She returned to Chicago brimming with determination and new ideas about labor. Soon after, a man named Terence Powderly spoke at a Knights of Labor meeting. Mary listened intently. When he'd finished, she began to call out questions from the audience. Before long the two were entertaining the crowd in an on-the-spot debate. Terence Powderly was impressed with Mary's knowledge of key issues affecting labor. After the program, they continued their animated talk.

As Mary increased her involvement in the labor movement, the United States was falling into a deep financial depression. By the end of 1873, many banks and businesses had failed. In all, over five thousand businesses closed. Many workers suffered wage cuts or lost their jobs entirely. Another financial panic in 1876 drove wages down again. Only one-fifth of the labor force worked full-time. Bands of impoverished, jobless people roamed the country looking for work, food, and housing.

Those people fortunate enough to keep their jobs or find new ones didn't want to complain to their employers. Labor unions began to lose members. By 1877, only eight or nine of the thirty national unions remained; membership dropped from three hundred thousand to fifty thousand.

Mary still believed in the importance of unions. She continued to work for the Knights of Labor, although she didn't agree with all of the organization's ideas. She had heard about a method of protest—striking—in which employees refused to work. At that time, the Knights of Labor believed that strikes couldn't be won. Mary didn't agree. She would try anything that might improve the daily lives of workers.

Having suffered the tragic loss of her family and survived the Great Chicago Fire, Mary had found a new purpose for her life. With the war to end slavery over, it was time to fight slavery in the workplace. That single purpose suited both her fiery spirit and her inborn sympathy for the downtrodden.

Mary Harris Jones had adopted America's workers as her family. In the future, they would call her Mother Jones.

"Cold as the breath of the wind of death are the Sad lessons that I learn," wrote Mary after the tragedies in her life. Instead of giving up, she found a new purpose: the fight for workers' rights.

*Railroad workers didn't share in the prosperity of railroad tycoons.
Many workers could barely feed their families.*

FOUR

Shutdown on the Railroad
1877–1886

A strike by railroad workers in 1877, which some called the "Great Upheaval," pulled forty-seven-year-old Mary into the middle of the first nationwide strike in U.S. history. The events that led up to the strike had spanned almost ten years. Since the Civil War, factories had grown, and so had the need to transport goods. Railroads had become the nation's largest and most profitable industry. Tycoons such as James Hill and Jay Gould had grown rich. Meanwhile, railroad workers often labored for fifteen to eighteen hours a day. They lived in shanties near the tracks. The five to ten dollars they made each week barely fed their families.

The situation for railroad workers grew even worse after the financial panics of 1873 and 1876. Railroad companies began to look for ways to keep profits high. On June 1, 1877, the Pennsylvania Railroad announced a ten percent cut in workers' wages. Three other major railroads quickly announced similar cuts. To trim costs further, the companies let trains, tracks, and trestle bridges fall into disrepair. Rusted boilers exploded and trestles collapsed. Some workers died.

The railroad companies had thoroughly angered their workers. No national railroad union existed yet, but scattered local strikes began in several states. On July 16 in Martinsburg, Virginia, more than twelve hundred brakemen and firemen for the Baltimore and Ohio Railroad walked off their jobs. They demanded that the company cancel its wage cuts. When police clashed with strikers who had massed on the tracks, President Rutherford B. Hayes sent in federal troops to restore order. Never before had the federal government gotten involved in a strike.

Strikers stopped the trains in Martinsburg, Virginia.

News of the Martinsburg rebellion traveled fast. Soon the strike spread to other states—Ohio, Missouri, Kentucky, Maryland, New York, New Jersey, Illinois, California, and Pennsylvania. Entire railroad lines shut down. Sympathetic citizens and workers from other trades joined the fight.

Within days, the Great Upheaval came to a head in Pittsburgh, Pennsylvania. When some Pittsburgh railroad workers asked Mary to come and help out during the strike there, she took one of the last trains out of Chicago before the railroads shut down.

Once in Pittsburgh, Mary didn't take a leading role in the strike but helped in any way she could. In the steaming July heat, she threaded her way through crowds of striking workers, encouraging them. She asked supporters of the strikers for money. She passed out leaflets to keep people informed about what was happening.

Shortly after Mary arrived, strikers and their supporters swarmed onto the tracks at the Pittsburgh train station, blocking all freight trains from passing. Local police could not control the mob. Finally, Pennsylvania's governor called in the state militia.

On July 21, about a week after the Great Upheaval had begun, soldiers carrying rifles with steel bayonets marched toward the crowds blocking the trains. Witnesses said some children threw stones at the soldiers. The soldiers immediately opened fire, killing twenty people and wounding twenty-nine. The crowd—close to twenty thousand people—flew into a rage. They forced the soldiers to take shelter in the roundhouse (a low, circular building where locomotives were kept).

Next, as Mary told it, "Hundreds of box cars standing on the tracks were soaked with oil and set on fire and sent down the tracks to the roundhouse." The roundhouse soon caught fire. Towering flames arched into the sky, fed by the oil-soaked cars. Fire wagons came, but the crowd kept the firefighters from dousing the flames.

The soldiers inside the roundhouse had few choices now. Some shot their way out. Flickering light glinted off their bayonets as they charged forward into the mob. Others tore off their shirts and fled out the back, hoping the mob outside wouldn't recognize them as soldiers.

Standing with other onlookers on a nearby hillside, Mary watched, probably as frightened as everyone else. By the time the fire was out, rioters had destroyed 79 buildings, 104 locomotives, and 2,152 railroad cars. Drunken looters caused another five to ten million dollars damage.

On August 2, 1877, the Great Upheaval ended in failure after federal troops moved in. Trains began rolling again. Railroad workers returned to their jobs to find their wages still cut and conditions almost unchanged.

The Great Upheaval marked a turning point in the labor movement. For the first time, federal troops had been called in to protect a big business, the railroad industry. From then on, many workers did not trust government. In addition, labor leaders now realized how easily mobs could get out of hand. Future strikes would have to be more strictly controlled.

The Great Upheaval had frightened company bosses and government officials. Legislators passed antilabor laws. States increased the size of their militias. Factories hired police to keep order. The public blamed the strikers—and workers in general—for the violence. Mary thought the other side was mostly responsible.

The Great Upheaval also marked a turning point in

Terence Powderly (standing, right) *at a Knights of Labor meeting. He described Mary as "a young seamstress . . . good looking, with a quick brain and an even quicker tongue."*

Mary's life. "From 1880 on, I became wholly engrossed in the labor movement," she wrote. She became a wanderer with no permanent address. To support herself, she may have worked as a seamstress. She also briefly managed a boardinghouse.

Meanwhile, her affection for Terence Powderly of the Knights of Labor grew. He was her dear friend rather than her political ally. Both cared deeply about America's workers, but the two disagreed about how to solve workers' problems.

Eleven people died in the riot in Haymarket Square.

Gentle and idealistic, Terence Powderly argued abstract ideas. Mary took action, even if that meant striking. A lawyer, Terence Powderly thought strikes were lawless and barbaric. Powderly held offices in both local and national governments. Mary distrusted most politicians.

Part of Mary's early education in strikes took place during the nationwide push to shorten the workday to eight hours. Support for a shorter workday had been growing since the early 1880s. Many labor groups supported this movement. So did Mary. She spoke at meetings and collected money for the cause.

A group of Chicago anarchists—people who wanted to get rid of all government—was also pushing for the shorter workday. Mary went to some of the anarchists' meetings, but she thought the radical group made the public too nervous and the police more savage.

On May 1, 1886, thousands of workers nationwide staged a peaceful demonstration for the eight-hour day. Two days later, a riot broke out at a Chicago industrial plant between strikers and strikebreakers. Police shot four workers.

To protest the police violence, twelve hundred people gathered the next day—May 4—at Haymarket Square in the center of Chicago's grimy lumber and packinghouse district. Just as police ordered the demonstrators to go home, a bomb exploded. Police swiftly opened fire on the crowd. By the time the flames and smoke cleared, seven policemen and four workers lay dead. One hundred people were wounded.

Newspaper stories quickly blamed the tragedy on the strikers. Distrustful of all labor groups now, the public called for justice. Eight anarchists were accused of starting the riot. Four were hung. One committed suicide. The other three served time in prison. Because of Haymarket Square, labor groups once again lost many members.

In Mary's view, "The workers asked only for bread and a shortening of the long hours of toil." For the moment, their hopes had died, drowned in the blood of Haymarket Square.

In narrow tunnels alongside underground ribbons of coal, boys tended the mules that pulled coal carts.

FIVE

"Suffer the Little Children"
1887–1894

By now a public image of Mary Harris Jones had formed. Increasingly, the nation's workers spotted her at labor meetings across the country, a small, sturdy woman, barely five feet tall. She had a direct, militant approach, though it was softened by her motherly manner and appearance. People rallied behind her like children following the Pied Piper. After 1890, people called her simply "Mother" Jones.

In 1890, the Knights of Labor joined forces with another union to form the United Mine Workers of America (UMW). Some 20,000 miners (out of 255,000 nationwide) belonged to the UMW by the end of the union's first year. Mother Jones moved from working for the Knights of Labor to working for the United Mine Workers as a paid organizer.

Mother Jones, now sixty-one, went to West Virginia in 1891 to help establish new UMW branches. There she glimpsed firsthand the cruel work of miners. Like coal miners all over the country, miners in West Virginia performed hard, brutal work. Mother Jones talked with men who worked fourteen hours a day, six days a week. Some tunnels alongside the seams—or underground ribbons—of coal were so narrow that the miners had to hunch over or even lie on their backs to dig out the coal. Sulfur water ate holes in their shoes and burned sores into their flesh.

Worse yet, cave-ins and explosions of underground gases regularly caused deaths. When the screeching mine whistle blew, signaling the start of another work shift, women sent their sons and husbands off to work never knowing if they'd see them alive again.

Mother Jones found herself drawn to these grime-smudged men. Young or old, miners were "boys" to her.

In the coal camps—towns where miners lived—families lived in flimsy shacks owned by the coal companies. Food and supplies could only be bought at company-owned stores, which charged high prices. People got their news from company-written newspapers. Children attended company-run schools.

Mother Jones took a train to Norton, West Virginia, where miners were on strike for better wages and working conditions. When she got off the train, miners told her the mine superintendent had threatened to "blow out her brains" unless she stayed away.

Though Mother Jones had never before taken an active role in a coal strike, she seemed to know how to answer. "You tell the superintendent that I am not coming to see him anyway," she said. "I am coming to see the miners." But because of this threat, she allowed an armed miner to accompany her whenever she went out alone.

When company officials refused to let her hold meetings on company land, members of a black congregation opened their doors to her. People flocked to the church to hear her. But before she began speaking, someone told her the church members might lose the use of their building because of her. She quickly canceled the meeting and sent her audience home. She later held her meeting on a public highway instead.

When mine guards chided her for allowing an armed miner to walk into "God's house," she answered, "Oh, that wasn't God's house. That is the coal company's house. Don't you know that God Almighty never comes around to a place like this!" Despite Mother Jones's efforts, the Norton strike failed in the end. Little changed for her "boys."

Three years later, Mother Jones became involved in another nationwide railroad strike. In 1893, a bold labor leader, Eugene Debs, pulled together separate groups of railroad workers—including brakemen, firemen, and porters—to form the American Railway Union. Before this, many of these groups had formed their own small unions. Using their combined power, the workers successfully fought the Great Northern Railway for better wages.

Then, in May 1894, they tackled the Pullman Palace Car Company. The company made elegant sleeping cars for trains. To protest the company's unfair treatment of its workers, members of the American Railway Union detached Pullman cars from trains and sidetracked the cars.

Soon the Pullman strike (nicknamed the "Debs Rebellion") grew. At that time, Mother Jones was in Birmingham, Alabama, working with a group of eight thousand coal miners who were protesting wage cuts. Violence broke out, and the governor called in the state militia. The miners decided to join the Pullman strike.

So did many other workers. Some 150,000 railroad workers walked off their jobs. Fifteen railroads shut down.

Federal troops moved the first train out of Chicago during the Pullman strike, a nationwide walkout by railroad workers.

Without trains to move goods and people, the country ground to a halt. A federal court issued a court order saying that goods and mail must be delivered. The trains must move. President Grover Cleveland called in federal troops to enforce the court order.

Like many other cities, Birmingham became an armed camp. Mother Jones "was forbidden to leave town without permit," she said, "forbidden to hold meetings." But she found ways to continue her work. "I slipped through the ranks of the soldiers without their knowing who I was," she said. Now sixty-four, she looked the part of "an old woman going to a missionary meeting to knit mittens."

The Pullman strike lasted from May to July 1894. Like the Great Upheaval and the Norton strike, it ended in failure.

Thirty strikers had died in the fighting that had broken out. Sixty others had been injured. Eugene Debs was jailed for defying the court order.

While Mother Jones was in Birmingham, she heard stories about horrible conditions in the South's cotton mills, where the region's vast supply of raw cotton was processed. To see if the stories were true, she went to Cottondale, Alabama, and got a job in one of the mills.

To get the job, she had to lie. At that time, cotton mills preferred to hire women with children so the whole family could work in the mill. Child labor was cheap. Mother Jones told the manager of the Cottondale mill that she had six children she'd left behind working on a farm. She had come ahead to find work before she sent for them. The manager was so delighted to hear this that he not only hired her, but also helped her look for a house to rent.

Mother Jones described the house he found for her as a "two-story plank shanty." It had broken windows, a front door that sagged open, holes in the roof, and rotten floorboards. She complained that the winter cold would seep through all the gaps. The manager told her she'd be thankful for those gaps when the steaming summer heat came.

In the mill, Mother Jones found conditions almost as bad as those under which black slaves had lived before the Civil War. Workers depended on the mill owner for housing; they purchased food at a company-owned store. Their meager wages barely lasted until the next payday.

But it was the children in the mill who tugged at Mother Jones's heart. At that time, few Southern states had laws protecting children. The textile industry used more child workers—most of them little girls—than any other industry in the country. Thirteen percent of workers in the cotton mills

Mill managers liked to hire families with children, since that meant more workers for the mill.

were children. Thirty percent of all workers in the South were children.

Mother Jones described children of six and seven "dragged out of bed at half past four in the morning when the task-master's whistle blew. They eat their scanty meals of black coffee and corn bread mixed with cottonseed oil in place of butter and then off trots the whole army of serfs, big and little." The children arrived at the mill where Mother Jones worked by 5:30 A.M. Inside, lung-choking lint filled the air. Many child workers suffered from bronchitis—an infection that causes deep coughing—or more serious lung diseases such as pneumonia and tuberculosis. Loud machines whirred and clacked. Mother Jones compared the sound to "iron rain" falling on the children's ears. At noon, workers stopped for a skimpy lunch and a brief half-hour rest. Then they continued without a break until the shift ended. Six-year-olds worked an eight-hour shift and earned ten cents a day.

At night, the youngest children were sometimes afraid to walk home in the dark, so they slept on the filthy factory floor. Those children who did trudge wearily home fell onto their beds of straw, too tired to eat or to take off their clothes. "Sleep was their recreation, their release, as play is to the free child," Mother Jones wrote. Yet when children fell asleep at the mill, the manager splashed cold water in their faces.

The children's suffering pained Mother Jones so deeply that she almost couldn't look at them. At least in the grim coalfields, grown men fought the labor battles—not these children with their sad faces and tired little bodies.

When Mother Jones's "six children" did not arrive, the manager grew suspicious that they didn't exist. So she moved on to Tuscaloosa, Alabama, and visited a rope factory. There, too, she found children at work. She described a man working a loom for forty cents a day. When she asked about his children, he pointed to two little girls with legs like twigs. Aged six and seven, the girls stood by a row of 155 spindles.

She said of these children, "Half-fed, half-clothed, half-housed, they toil on, while the poodle dogs of their masters are petted and coddled and sleep on pillows of down." At dawn, when children on the night shift left the rope factory, "they stumbled out of the heated atmosphere of the mill, shaking with cold as they came outside," according to Mother Jones. "They passed on their way home the long grey line of little children with their dinner pails coming in for the day's shift."

The supply of child workers seemed endless. Birth control methods were limited, so in many families, a new baby was almost always on the way. When child workers died of pneumonia and tuberculosis, "another little hand is ready to tie the snapped threads," Mother Jones wrote.

Mother Jones continued traveling through Alabama, Georgia, and South Carolina, finding work in mills and factories as she went along. In one South Carolina textile mill, she observed overworked, underfed pregnant women who gave birth and, within hours, went back to work. Their newborn babies lay in boxes on the floor beside the mothers' looms. Older babies crawled in the dirt and lint on the floor or toddled in and out of the "forests" of heavy spindles.

In Gibson, Tennessee, Mother Jones found such bleak conditions that she called Gibson "another of those little sections of hell with which the South is covered." Most people worked in a mill that wove gingham cloth. One Gibson resident told Mother Jones that she earned a dollar each week at the mill. With it she bought enough food at the "pluck-me" company store to last until the next payday. At the end of a long year's work, she had saved only one dollar.

In one mill town, a family had run up a debt of thirty-six dollars when the father became ill and died. The mother and her three children all worked. But after they paid for rent, food, and the interest charged on the money they owed, no money remained. They had no hope of repaying the debt or being able to save enough money so they could leave.

Mother Jones decided to help them escape. She borrowed a wagon from a farmer and greased the axles so they wouldn't squeak. Then she convinced some railroad workers she knew to make an unscheduled stop that night at the station in town. In the dark, Mother Jones drove the family to the station. Everyone jumped at the slightest shadow. Mother Jones said they felt like runaway slaves, two steps ahead of the slave catchers and the bloodhounds.

As the train pulled in, its lone headlight looked like a huge, glaring eye lighting up the dark tracks. The children shrank back, whimpering. Once on board, the mother and her children broke into tears of relief. As the train sped off, Mother Jones hoped the family could make a new start without "the millstone [of debt] around their neck."

Everywhere Mother Jones went, she was horrified by the dismal lives child workers led. "Their little lives are woven into the cotton goods they weave," she wrote. "In that thread are twisted the tears and heart-ache of little children."

In one of many speeches Mother Jones made on the evils of child labor, she quoted a Bible verse in which Jesus said, "Suffer the little children to come unto me…for of such is the kingdom of God" (Mark 10:14). Maybe the children Mother Jones knew did belong to the "kingdom of God." But she added, "If Heaven is full of undersized, round shouldered, hollow-eyed, listless, sleepy little angel children, I want to go to the other place with the bad little boys and girls."

"I work for the children unborn," Mother Jones said. "No children in the mines and mills of the future is my cry."

SIX

"Boys, Listen to Me"

1894–1899

After studying Southern cotton mills, Mother Jones went to New York City. Her memories of the fragile child workers haunted her. "For a long time after my southern experience, I could scarcely eat," she wrote. "Not alone my clothes, but my food, too, at times seemed bought with the price of the toil of children."

What she'd seen in the South had also started Mother Jones thinking about an economic system called socialism. She had read about socialist ideas in a new newspaper, *Appeal to Reason.* Socialists believed the government—not private citizens—should run industries such as railroads, coal mines, and cotton mills. The United States economy operated under capitalism, a system of private ownership and free trade with little government interference. Mother Jones thought socialism might improve the lives of workers. A socialist government, she reasoned, might give the owners of companies less control over people's lives.

Mother Jones began selling subscriptions to *Appeal to Reason,* which was popular in the Midwest and the South. In

Omaha, Nebraska, she sold this socialist newspaper to soldiers in military barracks. "Soldiers are the sons of working people, and need to know it," she said.

Mother Jones also wrote articles for the *Appeal.* She and other writers offered simple answers to the problems of the working poor. The *Appeal's* articles were easy to read, its pages filled with jokes, recipes, and strike news. Cartoons showed silk-hatted factory owners stealing money out of workers' pockets.

The paper also carried reading lists, which Mother Jones liked, since she believed workers needed to educate themselves. She once told a crowd, "Boys, listen to me. Instead of going to the pool and gambling rooms, go up to the mountain and read this book. Sit under the trees, listen to the birds, and take a lesson from those little feathered creatures who do not exploit one another."

Although Mother Jones considered herself a socialist, she didn't pay much attention to socialist philosophy. Ideas meant less to her than action. She was "not *for* the revolution, but *in* it." She liked to be on the move, flitting from one labor group or fight to another, like a butterfly. When the heart of the action moved somewhere else, off she flew.

During the Pullman strike, Mother Jones and Eugene Debs had become friends. Since then, Debs had become a leader in the socialist movement. In 1896, Debs went to Birmingham, and Mother Jones went there to help him. She passed out leaflets and urged miners to come hear Debs speak at the opera house in Birmingham.

On the Sunday when Debs was to speak, city officials banned the meeting. Boldly, Mother Jones got a group of miners to carry Debs on their shoulders through the streets of Birmingham, right past the offices of the mayor and the chief of police. The officials changed their minds and let Debs speak.

Several months later, Mother Jones joined Debs at a labor conference in Wheeling, West Virginia. West Virginia had some of the richest coal mines—and some of the poorest coal miners—in the country. She and other prominent labor leaders hoped to help the United Mine Workers gain a foothold in West Virginia. On July 27, 1897, they spoke to crowds as large as seventeen thousand.

Three weeks before the conference, twenty thousand West Virginia miners had joined a nationwide strike to protest wage cuts in the mines. Coal companies responded by bringing in special detectives to face down the strikers and protect strikebreakers. Those miners who stayed on the job got increased wages and bonuses. Miners who joined the strikers were immediately fired.

Mother Jones and socialist leader Eugene Debs were friends.

Crowds in West Virginia listened intently to Mother Jones.

Mother Jones, now sixty-seven, flew into action. With no paychecks coming in, the strikers' most urgent need was for food. Mother Jones got farmers in northern West Virginia to donate produce. She organized "pound parties"—women volunteers brought a pound of food to share with the strikers. She gathered strikers' wives into picket lines to frighten away strikebreakers. She led fifty little girls in a parade. They carried banners that read "Our Papas Aren't Scared." And she convinced factory workers to come to meetings and to donate food and money to the cause. Despite her efforts and those of Eugene Debs and other leaders, the twelve-week strike ended in failure in September 1897.

Another event during this period deeply impressed Mother Jones. Some mine bosses in Illinois refused to give miners the wages they had promised in an earlier agreement, so the miners went on strike. Then the companies tried to replace the miners with black strikebreakers from Alabama, who would work for lower wages. When a trainload of strikebreakers—protected by heavily armed guards—steamed into the town of Virden, Illinois, angry miners filled the streets. A fierce battle took place as the train neared the stockade that the Chicago–Virden Coal Company had built around its mine to protect the strikebreakers. Mine guards and miners began shooting at each other. Fourteen miners and five guards were killed. Several more people on both sides were wounded. Labor leaders called the event a massacre.

Undaunted, the Virden miners kept up the pressure for several more months. Angrily, they destroyed the company store. Illinois's governor called in the national guard to prevent more strikebreakers from being unloaded. This was the first time troops had been used to defend the rights of workers. Finally, after six months, the company hired back the miners.

Mother Jones admired the courage of the Virden miners, especially those who had died. So did many others. To honor the victims of the Virden massacre, a group of miners created a cemetery for union miners in Mount Olive, Illinois. Mother Jones asked to be buried there. And in many labor battles to come, "Remember Virden!" became the union's rallying cry.

Mother Jones willingly shared the lives of poor mining families in Pennsylvania.

SEVEN

An Army of Women with Mops and Brooms

1899–1900

In 1899, Mother Jones, now seventy, went to the anthracite—or hard coal—fields of eastern Pennsylvania. With her were William Wilson and Thomas Haggerty (two founders of the UMW) and several other organizers. Their job was to convince miners to join the union. Haggerty became one of Mother Jones's favorite coworkers.

Anthracite was the main fuel in the eastern United States. Conditions in the dark, dank mines where it was dug were some of the most dangerous in the world. Hunched in narrow tunnels four hundred feet below ground, miners hacked the hard coal out of the earth. Seeping groundwater drenched them, causing sores and disease. Coal dust swirled around them, slowly poisoning their lungs.

From 1876 to 1897, some 7,346 men died in mining-related accidents in eastern Pennsylvania. The men worked under the threat of instant death from cave-ins or gas explosions underground. For this dangerous work, coal miners earned a dollar and a half—or less—for a fourteen-hour shift.

Worse yet, in Pennsylvania (as in the rest of the nation), one-sixth of the miners were under the age of fourteen. The youngest workers earned the lowest wages—well under a dollar a day. Nationwide, as many as twenty-five thousand boys under sixteen worked in mines and quarries. The boys held jobs above and below ground, but most were "breaker boys."

Breakers were huge buildings built into the sides of hills or mountains where coal was prepared for shipment. As coal came rattling down a chute, breaker boys perched on ladders on either side of the chute and separated pieces of slate and debris from the coal. The boys breathed in coal dust. Their

Breaker boys separated debris and slate from the chunks of coal.

shoulders grew rounded from bending over the chute. Their fingers were cut or broken by jagged rocks. Some boys fell into the chute and were crushed to death. If the boys didn't work fast enough, the breaker boss rapped their knuckles. "The fingers of the little boys bled, bled on to the coal. Their nails were out to the quick," Mother Jones wrote.

Underground, young "trapper boys" tended the mules that hauled the coal. Trapper boys worked fourteen hours a day. They stood in mud up to their ankles in the dark mine tunnels, seeing only mules and rats. Mother Jones said no sunshine ever came into these children's lives.

Some trapper boys were only nine or ten years old.

The homes of many mining families were little more than shacks.

Mother Jones hiked the hills and valleys of Pennsylvania as a delegate for the UMW. She went to stores, fields, and taverns where miners gathered. She introduced herself with a firm handshake. Miners told her their stories. In turn, she preached about the union. When interest was strong, she held meetings, usually at night and away from the mine. She peppered her speeches with humor and dramatized real-life stories. Her message was simple: Joining the union offered the only chance for a better life.

Dressed in her trademark black dresses and wearing hip boots, she tramped along railroad tracks and dirt roads. When trains came by, she flagged them down for free rides to the coal camps. Other times she climbed rugged mountains. Sometimes coworkers carried her across icy streams to reach the camps. Saying she liked to travel light, she wrapped everything she owned in a little bundle. She once said an extra dress was a burden, too much to carry.

Mother Jones loved the brave, hardy mountain women who shared their flimsy shacks with her as she traveled from camp to camp. Some women were immigrants from Italy, Ireland, and Poland. Others came from families that had lived in the Appalachian Mountains for generations.

Mother Jones willingly took part in the harsh lives these poor women lived. She ate the meager meals they prepared. She curled up at night with their children, shivering when there wasn't enough coal for the stove. Or she slept on a bare floor with her purse for a pillow. She gave away any extra money she had.

When word came of an explosion in the mine tunnels, Mother Jones stood with the wives at the mine gate, waiting to hear about their husbands. When bad news came, she helped prepare the dead for burial.

Nearly a thousand coal miners had begun a strike in May 1899 in Arnot, Pennsylvania. They wanted wage increases from the Erie Company, which owned several small mines in the Arnot area. By late September, mining families were struggling to survive without pay. The miners decided to give up the strike. The new UMW president, John Mitchell, asked Mother Jones to go to Arnot to encourage the miners to continue.

On the day before the miners planned to return to their jobs, Mother Jones arrived before dawn at a train station near Arnot. A young boy named William Bouncer met her. Bundled into his buggy, the two bumped along rough roads for most of the sixteen miles to Arnot.

"It was biting cold," Mother Jones wrote later. As the sun rose, she watched the mist clear above trees splashed with the gold and red colors of fall. Low mountain ridges spread into the valleys like outstretched fingers. When she arrived in Arnot, she took a room at the town's only hotel, which was owned by the coal company. That afternoon she held a meeting with the miners and their families.

"Rise and pledge to stick to your brothers and the union till the strike's won!" she said in a low, firm voice. The men shuffled their feet and mumbled to each other. But the miners' wives pledged to make sure that no one returned to work in the morning. Mother Jones called another meeting for the next day.

That night, Mother Jones heard a knock on her hotel room door. The housekeeper had come to tell her that she must leave the hotel. Coal company bosses had heard about the upcoming meeting and had ordered her out. Young Bouncer was downstairs, standing guard. In the dark, the boy drove the weary Mother Jones up the mountain. A cold wind almost blew her lace-trimmed bonnet off her head. He took her to the tarpaper shack of one of the mining families. There, she and the miner's wife slept in the family's only bed. The miner dozed at the kitchen table.

The next morning, company officials arrived. They said the whole family must leave because they had helped Mother Jones. The mother, father, and children hurriedly gathered up their belongings. They piled their few sticks of furniture, scattered clothes, and pictures into a wagon. Then they walked with Mother Jones to the meeting. Word spread that the family—and Mother Jones—had been turned out of their house. Angry now, the miners voted to continue their strike.

The company brought in strikebreakers. Mother Jones decided to get the miners' wives to chase the strikebreakers away from one of the mines, Drip Mouth. She told the

Like these Ohio miners, angry miners in Pennsylvania voted to continue striking.

women to come armed with mops, brooms, pots, and pans. Nursing mothers could bring their babies with them. Older children should stay home with the men.

Mother Jones knew that if she led this "women's army" herself, police would arrest her. She didn't fear jail, but she knew the union needed her. So she chose a large Irishwoman to lead the charge.

On the day of the "battle," the Irishwoman arrived wearing a petticoat hastily thrown over a thick cotton nightgown. She had flyaway red hair and wore one white stocking, one black stocking, and sturdy shoes. Mother Jones eyed the

Mother Jones organized a women's army like this one.

woman's flushed complexion and wild appearance. "I looked at her and felt that she could raise a rumpus," Mother Jones said. The other women were also wearing their hair loose and were dressed in an assortment of rags.

"Take that tin dishpan . . . and your hammer," Mother Jones said to the Irishwoman, "and when the scabs and the mules come up, begin to hammer and howl and be ready to chase the scabs with your mops and brooms. Don't be afraid of anyone."

The women marched up the mountain to the mine entrance, howling, screaming, and banging on their pots and pans. The Arnot sheriff tapped the thickset leader of the march on the shoulder and asked her not to frighten the mules used to haul the coal cars. The Irishwoman wheeled around and smacked him on the head with her tin pan. Sure enough, the mules snorted in fear, broke away from their drivers, and galloped off. Then, brandishing mops and brooms, the women chased the scabs down the hill.

For many days after that, the miners' wives patrolled the entrance to the Drip Mouth mine around the clock. They held their babies in one arm, their mops and brooms in the other. To pass the time, they sang. At night, they huddled in the frosty cold, peering through the darkness to make sure no scabs sneaked past the gate.

Meanwhile, Mother Jones urged miners in the camps around Arnot to stand firm. With a miner's young son as her driver, she traveled from camp to camp in a mule-drawn wagon. It was a rugged way to travel for a seventy-year-old woman in midwinter.

She talked to the miners, using their own rough language. As one coal miner wrote, "The miners knew and respected her. They might think it a little queer perhaps—it *was* an odd kind of work for a woman in those days—but they knew she was a good soul. . . . She had a lively sense of humor—she could tell wonderful stories, usually at the expense of some boss, for she couldn't resist the temptation to agitate, even in a joke—and she exuded a warm friendliness and human sympathy."

Sometimes she even warmed up a crowd by playing music on a windup phonograph. "I play all kinds of comic pieces and get the crowd in a good humor," she said in a letter to John Mitchell.

The work was exhausting. "Sometimes it was twelve or one o'clock in the morning when I would get home. The little boy asleep on my arm and I driving the mule," wrote Mother Jones. "Sometimes it was several degrees below zero. The winds whistled down the mountains and drove the snow and sleet in our faces. My hands and feet were often numb. We were all living on dry bread and black coffee. I slept in a room that never had a fire in it, and I often woke up in the morning to find snow covering the outside covers of the bed."

Encouraging the miners wasn't her only task; food and housing for the families were constant needs. The mine bosses had offered to pay local farmers if they refused to help the striking miners. But Mother Jones talked the farmers into feeding the children and letting homeless families stay on the farms.

Finally, in February 1900, the Erie Company agreed to the miners' demand for better wages. The strike had lasted ten long months. One UMW official gave most of the credit to Mother Jones. He said she had "snatched victory out of the very jaws of defeat." Miners held a farewell party to honor Mother Jones and to celebrate the end of the strike. As blizzard winds blasted snow in their faces, the men, women, and children of the Arnot area walked to the opera house in the nearby town of Blossburg.

"It was one night of real joy and a great celebration," said Mother Jones. Children raced up to the sweet-faced, white-haired woman and kissed her hands. Men cracked open some nearby freight cars and helped themselves to the crates of beer inside. People talked and sang the whole night long.

Despite the victory at Arnot, more trouble broke out in the anthracite mines of eastern Pennsylvania in the fall of 1900. This time the strike was much more widespread, involving 120,000 coal miners working for several different companies. Almost ninety percent of Pennsylvania's anthracite mines shut down. The miners had three key demands: a ten percent wage increase, no more company stores, and improvements in working conditions.

Mother Jones held meetings all over the area, urging miners to join the union and support the strike. She led a group of three thousand women in a march from the town of McAdoo over the mountains to Coaldale, where miners had resisted joining the union. The marchers beat on tin pans, waved brooms and American flags, and shouted "Join the union! Join the union!"

What happened next isn't clear. According to Mother Jones, her "pots and pans" brigade "mopped up Coaldale," convincing most of the miners to join the union. But long after the event, historians questioned how effective she really had been.

After six weeks, the anthracite strike ended in October 1900. The coal companies grudgingly gave the miners the ten percent wage increase, but nothing else. Because of the work done by Mother Jones, John Mitchell, and other labor leaders, membership in the United Mine Workers swelled from eight thousand members at the strike's beginning to one hundred thousand by the end of the year.

Mother Jones was now known as one of the most successful—and one of the most colorful—organizers in the country. This made her increasingly unpopular with company bosses. She had discovered an important tool in the fight for miners' rights—women. Of these women with their mops and brooms, she said, "They were fighting for the advancement of a great country." She felt they had played an important role in the victory at Arnot and in the larger strike that followed.

She wrote later, "An army of strong mining women makes a wonderfully spectacular picture."

In the coal camps of West Virginia, coal companies controlled nearly everything in a child's life.

EIGHT

Trouble in West Virginia
1901–1903

"**M**edieval West Virginia!" Mother Jones once said. "With its tent colonies on the bleak hills! With its grim men and women! When I get to the other side, I shall tell God Almighty about West Virginia!"

Over a period of almost thirty years, Mother Jones returned again and again to West Virginia to try to get miners to join the United Mine Workers. She made some of her most fiery speeches in that state. On several occasions, she spent time in jail. In the fall of 1901 and the spring of 1902, she was put in charge of spreading the union's message in the coalfields in the southern part of the state.

Clusters of mines filled every cove and hollow of this mountainous state. The bituminous—or soft coal—seams were unusually rich and thick, some six to ten feet wide. Because the state was so mountainous, miners lived cut off from each other.

As in other mining states, young boys worked as breaker boys and trapper boys. The coal companies nearly controlled people's whole lives in company-built towns. As one historian

71

put it, "Boys were brought into the world by the company doctor, attended the company schools. . . grew into manhood and worked in the company breaker or washery, and finally were buried by the company undertaker."

West Virginia mine owners paid the lowest wages in the country. Miners received about forty-three cents for each ton of coal they dug—an average of $275 a year. In Indiana, miners earned more than double that, at eighty-eight cents per ton. Instead of a paycheck, miners received scrip, a piece of paper they could use only at company stores, where prices were inflated. When mine bosses figured out how much scrip a miner was owed, they first deducted expenses. As Mother Jones explained it, "[Credit for] two tons of coal must go to the company each year for house rent; two tons to the company doctor. . . . Two tons more for the water which they use." She wasn't surprised when miners looked as if "there was nothing on earth to live for."

Coal companies paid miners scrip instead of real money. Scrip could only be spent in stores owned by the company.

Mr. _____

BALANCE DUE WORKMAN $ _____

LAUREL SMOKELESS COAL CO.

By Tons Cwt.			To Store Account	
" "			" Balance	
" Yards @			" Rent	
" " @			" Coal	
" Slate			" Smithing	
" Days @			" Labor	
" " @			" Cash Advanced	
" Month's Salary			" Doctor	
" Cks. Returned			" Burial Fund	
" Labor @			" Checks	
			" Insurance	
Cash held last day to Balance			" Hospital	
Account			" Lights	
			Check off	
			O. A. P.	
			U. I.	
Total Earnings			Total Debit	
By Balance Due Workman			To Bal. Due Co.	

Received of _____ No. _____
LAUREL SMOKELESS COAL COMPANY
DOLLARS _____ in full of all claims to and including

CENTS

Witness at Signing _____

Sign Here _____
Paragon Print. 2M 9-38 100884

This balance sheet shows what one miner earned (on the left) and what he owed the company (on the right). After a month's work, he owed more than he had earned.

In spite of these harsh conditions, the United Mine Workers fought an uphill battle in West Virginia. Miners were fearful of joining the union. Of the state's 23,000 miners, only 206 belonged to the union.

Mother Jones, now seventy-two, worked with other UMW organizers, including Thomas Haggerty and young John Walker from Illinois. She and Walker formed a close, warm friendship. They sometimes tramped five to twenty miles up mountains to talk with the miners. At night, as they approached a meeting place, the lights of twinkling stars mingled with the lights of miners' lamps. People came from all over to hear her speak.

Mother Jones sprinkled swear words and her own brand of religion into her speeches. She said swearing was the way working people prayed, especially when they wanted a fast answer. She'd tell the miners to buy guns to protect themselves from the "god damn guards." But in the next breath, she'd mention "the Almighty" to make a point.

When miners wanted to meet in a church, Mother Jones told them a church was a "praying institution" and a union was a "fighting institution." So she held meetings in open fields instead. She told the miners, "Pray for the dead and fight like hell for the living!"

Mother Jones had a spellbinding impact on crowds. Many people said they could listen to her talk all night. She told stories filled with details out of their own lives, then added in her low, tense voice, "I am one of you, and I know what it is to suffer." She blasted mine owners and scolded those workers unwilling or too frightened to join the union and fight for their rights. But "lickspittles" (as she called scabs and mine guards) made her the maddest of all.

During this period, she wrote regularly to John Mitchell, the UMW's young president, and also to its secretary, William Wilson. Colorful details about her activities, union politics, and the weather filled her long, rambling letters. "My boys are doing good work," she told Mitchell. Sometimes she scribbled a note asking for money. She misspelled or left out words. She forgot punctuation marks and capital letters, as if she were writing in haste. Her large handwriting sprawled across union or hotel stationery. She signed her letters simply "Mother."

She had an unbending rule about any of her fellow organizers drinking. "Every move must be strictly business," she explained. Coworkers tried to meet her standards and avoid her anger. But Mother Jones didn't think all drinking was wrong. She defended people's right to gather at saloons.

After speaking for two or three hours, union organizers often walked home in the middle of the night. Trudging along the railroad tracks after meetings, Mother Jones often counted the rails to keep herself awake. When roads flooded, she and other union workers slogged miles through knee-high mud to get to the more remote camps. "I had a frightful walk last night in mud and rained like fury. . . . After hiking long, my poor feet are so sore," she wrote Mitchell. Once a poisonous copperhead snake almost bit her.

Still, she vowed she wouldn't trade her situation for anything. "Who would not tramp for the young boys and break their chains? . . . " she said. "My heart goes out to these boys."

Mine owners often made it hard for organizers to hire halls for meetings or to rent hotel rooms. One coal company told Mother Jones she couldn't even pass out leaflets to announce a meeting in its town. But Mother Jones sent two men into the town with a clever plan. The two wandered along the town's streets, pretending one of them was hard of hearing. The first man said loudly, "Mother Jones is going to have a meeting Sunday afternoon outside the town on the sawdust pile!" When the second man pretended not to hear, his companion shouted even more loudly. Word of the meeting soon spread through the mining camp. Mother Jones had her crowd.

By February 1902, when Mother Jones had been in West Virginia several months, she wrote to William Wilson, "I feel that there is a ray of sunshine breaking for those so long in bondage." In the region where Mother Jones had been working, her efforts paid off. Two new local branches of the union formed in the Kanawha River valley. In Thurmond, a crowd of three hundred miners met her train, clasped her hands, and asked her to stay with them. "They had their UMW buttons on and were not afraid or ashamed to wear it," she told Wilson. Because of her efforts, she felt these men now realized they had rights worth fighting for.

On the other hand, little progress had been made in the northern coalfields. The Fairmont Coal Company controlled all the major fields for fifteen miles along the West Fork River near Fairmont. The Clarksburg Fuel Company controlled the mines in the hills near Clarksburg.

In March 1902, the union asked these powerful companies for a fixed scale of wages, but the companies refused. Their profits were rising, and they knew that many miners still resisted joining the union. In May, UMW president John Mitchell asked Mother Jones to go to the northern coalfields, where he felt she could do the most good.

On June 7, the UMW called a statewide strike for better wages and shorter hours. Nearly sixteen thousand miners in twenty-five West Virginia counties left their jobs. The day after the strike began, Mother Jones took part in a thirty-mile march from Flemington to Grafton in the heart of the Fairmont Coal Company holdings. Several hundred people came to hear her speak at a school near the strikers' camp. The sheriff later arrested strike leader Thomas Haggerty for his part in the mass demonstration and banned further meetings in the area. Mother Jones took over as strike leader.

One night, Mother Jones was on her way to a meeting outside Fairmont. She had arranged to meet three other organizers—including a man named Joe Battley—near a bridge where the interurban trolley stopped. As Mother Jones waited in the darkness, she saw shadowy shapes on the bridge. Then she heard running footsteps. Suddenly voices screamed, "Murder! Murder! Police! Help!" Thugs were attacking Joe Battley, the voices shouted. Mother Jones knew the trolley was due. She ran toward the bridge and shouted, "Joe! Joe! The boys are coming. The whole bunch's coming! The car's almost here!"

Fooled into thinking an army of miners was arriving on the trolley, the attackers fled. "They left Joe on the bridge, his head broken, and the blood pouring from him," said Mother Jones. She tore her petticoat into strips and bandaged the man's head. It took weeks for him to recover.

Mother Jones traveled next to a mine near Parkersburg to hold a meeting. She knew that mine owners had gotten a judge in Parkersburg to ban all gatherings of strikers. She went ahead with her meeting anyway.

While Mother Jones was in West Virginia, she wrote long, rambling letters to John Mitchell. "My boys are doing good work," she said, or, "Send me some money."

On the afternoon of June 20, she spoke bitterly about Judge John Jay Jackson and called the mine owners "robbers." In the middle of her speech, a federal marshal sent a man up to the platform to tell her that she was under arrest for going against the judge's court order. Eyeing the marshal, she said calmly, "I will be right with you. Wait 'til I run down," and finished speaking. In parting, she said to the crowd, "Goodbye boys; I'm under arrest. I may have to go to jail. I may not see you for a long time. Keep up this fight!" Then she called the judge a "scab."

The marshal arrested Mother Jones and eleven other organizers. Guards tried to take Mother Jones to a hotel instead of to the jail. She snapped that she wasn't going to a hotel while some of her boys were in jail. But at the jailer's insistence, she stayed with him and his wife in their quarters. They "treated me as a member of the family," Mother Jones wrote, "getting out the best of everything. . . . I got a real good rest when I was with them."

At Mother Jones's trial, the prosecutor called her "the most dangerous woman in the country today." Judge Jackson hinted he would release Mother Jones if she abandoned her strike activities and left the state for good. She said all the "devils in hell" couldn't make her give up.

Surprisingly, he released her anyway. Free on bail until her trial was set to continue, she traveled to Indiana to attend a UMW convention. The union had to decide where to spend its time and money. Many members wanted to concentrate on the anthracite strike going on in Pennsylvania rather than join the fight in West Virginia.

Mother Jones talked about the struggles of the West Virginia miners. She urged the convention to fight in both states. "It matters not whether a miner is robbed in Illinois

One of Mother Jones's strongest beliefs was that miners of all races should stick together.

or in Virginia, in Indiana or in the anthracite region," she said. "They are all ours, and we must fight the battle for all of them."

She also tackled a tough subject—black strikebreakers. Mine owners often rounded up black workers from the South and brought them in as strikebreakers. Many of the black workers didn't know they'd been hired to replace strikers. The practice made miners angry; some threatened to hang the strikebreakers.

Even though Mother Jones hated scabs herself, she wanted to remind the miners not to blame all black workers.

"One of the best fellows we have is the black man, . . . " she said. "He knows what liberty is; he knows that in days gone by the bloodhounds went after his father over the mountains and tore him to pieces, and he knows that his Mammy wept and prayed for liberty. For these reasons, he prizes his liberty and is ready to fight for it." To Mother Jones's disappointment, the convention threw most of its financial support to the Pennsylvania strikers, leaving those in West Virginia on their own.

Boasting that she was not afraid to go to jail, Mother Jones returned to West Virginia for her trial. Judge Jackson made no secret of his sympathy for the mine owners. On July 24, he sentenced most of the strike leaders to sixty days in jail. Thomas Haggerty got ninety days.

But the judge told Mother Jones she was free to go. He didn't want Mother Jones to use jail to whip up public sympathy. He said he hoped she had learned from the experience. He sounded surprised that a woman of her intelligence would do some of the things she'd done. Warning her not to take part in any more strikes, he suggested charity work as a better use of her time.

Firmly, Mother Jones told the judge she must continue her union work. She added that they were both old and didn't have long to live. She hoped that they would die good friends and that they would meet in heaven. The judge's response brought applause and laughter from the audience. He hinted that he and Mother Jones probably wouldn't meet in the afterlife; the two of them weren't likely to end up in the same place.

Mother Jones briefly joined the anthracite strike in Pennsylvania. In a behind-the-scenes deal with John Mitchell, President Theodore Roosevelt finally settled the strike.

Miners won some but not all of their damands. Mother Jones thought John Mitchell had given in too easily. She also thought Mitchell spent too much time relaxing in hotels and not enough time out in the field.

Mother Jones returned to West Virginia that fall with John Walker. They encouraged strikers in the New River and Kanawha River valley coalfields. "The work was not easy or safe and I was lucky to have so fearless a co-worker," she said of Walker. They led meetings at night in the woods, in barns, or in abandoned mines.

"Often after meetings in this mountain district, we sat through the night on the river bank," she wrote. "Frequently we would hear bullets whizz past us as we sat huddled between boulders, our black clothes making us invisible in the blackness of the night."

Even without the UMW's backing, the West Virginia strikers held on into 1903. But the mine owners stood firm. Men who joined the union were blacklisted (denied work) or bushwhacked (shot in a surprise attack). When seven miners were brutally murdered at a coal camp near Stanaford Mountain, Mother Jones comforted their widows and children.

Despite the work of Mother Jones and others, the 1902–1903 strike in West Virginia failed. Wages remained lower, the workday longer, and the cost of living higher than in other states. Many local branches of the union disbanded.

The strike's one success came in the Kanawha River valley, largely due to the efforts of Mother Jones. There, some seven thousand miners won improvements in working conditions as well as a shorter workday—nine hours instead of twelve to fourteen. It would be ten years before another major strike took place in West Virginia. Mother Jones would be there.

"I've got stock in these little children," Mother Jones said of
young mill workers like these girls.

NINE

The March of the Mill Children

1903

"I love children," Mother Jones once told a reporter. In countless shacks and shanties across the country, she had tied the shoes of children, wiped their noses, hugged them when they cried, scrambled to find food for them, fought for their rights. By the turn of the century, almost two million children under the age of sixteen worked in mills, factories, and mines. Images of the child workers Mother Jones had seen stayed with her—the torn, bleeding fingers of the breaker boys, the mill children living on coffee and stale bread.

In June 1903, Mother Jones went to Philadelphia, Pennsylvania—the heart of a vast textile industry. About one hundred thousand workers from six hundred different mills were on strike there. The strikers wanted their workweek cut from sixty to fifty-five hours, even if it meant lower wages. About a sixth of the strikers were children under sixteen.

Nationwide, eighty thousand children worked in the textile industry. In the South, Mother Jones had seen how dangerous their jobs were. Barefooted little girls and boys reached their tiny hands into the treacherous machinery to repair snapped threads or crawled underneath the machinery to oil it. At textile union headquarters, Mother Jones met more of these mill children. Their bodies were bone-thin, with hollow chests. Their shoulders were rounded from long hours spent hunched over the workbenches. Even worse, she saw "some with their hands off, some with the thumb missing, some with their fingers off at the knuckles"—victims of mill accidents.

Pennsylvania, like many other states, had laws that said children under thirteen could not work. But parents often lied about a child's age. Poor families either put their children to work in the mills or starved. Mill owners looked the other way, because child labor was cheap.

Mother Jones asked various newspaper publishers why they didn't write about child labor in Pennsylvania. The publishers told her they couldn't, since owners of the mills also owned stock in their newspapers. "Well, I've got stock in these little children," she said, "and I'll arrange a little publicity."

Mother Jones, now seventy-three, gathered a large group of mill children and their parents. She led them on a one-mile march from Philadelphia's Independence Square to its courthouse lawn. Mother Jones and a few children climbed up on a platform in front of a huge crowd. She held one boy's arm up high so the crowd could see his mutilated hand. "Philadelphia's mansions were built on the broken bones, the quivering hearts, and drooping heads of these children," she said. She lifted another child in her arms so the crowd could see how thin he was.

Mother Jones looked directly at the city officials standing at the open windows across the street. "Some day the workers will take possession of your city hall, and when we do, no child will be sacrificed on the altar of profit." Unmoved, the officials quickly closed their windows.

Local newspapers and some New York newspapers covered the event. How, Mother Jones wondered, could she draw national attention to the evils of child labor? Philadelphia's famous Liberty Bell, currently on a national tour and drawing huge crowds, gave her an idea. She and the textile union leaders would stage their own tour. They would march the mill children all the way to the president of the United States—Theodore Roosevelt. Mother Jones wanted the president to get Congress to pass a law that would take children out of the mills, mines, and factories, and put them in school.

When Mother Jones asked parents for permission to take their children with her, many hesitated. The march from Philadelphia to Sagamore Hill—the president's seaside mansion on Long Island near New York City—would cover 125 miles. It would be a difficult journey. But finally, the parents agreed. Many decided to come along on the march. Other striking men and women offered their help, too.

On July 7, 1903, nearly three hundred men, women, and children—followed by four wagons with supplies—began the long march. Newspapers carried daily reports of the march, calling the group "Mother Jones's Industrial Army," or "Mother Jones's Crusaders." The army was led by a fife-and-drum corps of three children dressed in Revolutionary War uniforms. Mother Jones wore her familiar, lace-fringed black dress. The marchers sang and carried flags, banners, and placards that read "We Want to Go to School!" "We Want Time to Play." "Prosperity Is Here. Where Is Ours?" "55 Hours or Nothing." "We Only Ask for Justice." "More School, Less Hospitals."

The temperature rose into the nineties. The roads were dusty, the children's shoes full of holes. Many of the young girls returned home. Some of the marchers walked only as far as the outskirts of Philadelphia. For the hundred or so marchers who remained, this trip was an adventure in spite

When young textile workers began a march with Mother Jones in 1903, newspapers called them "Mother Jones's Industrial Army."

of the heat. They bathed and swam in brooks and rivers. Each of them carried a knapsack with a knife, fork, tin cup, and plate inside. Mother Jones took a huge pot for cooking meals on the way. Mother Jones also took along costumes, makeup, and jewelry so the children could stop in towns along the route and put on plays about the struggles of textile workers. The fife-and-drum corps gave concerts and passed the hat. People listened and donated money. Farmers met the marchers with wagonloads of fruits, vegetables, and clothes. Railroad engineers stopped their trains and gave them free rides. Hotel owners served free meals.

On July 10, the marchers camped across the Delaware River from Trenton, New Jersey. They had traveled about forty miles in three days. At first, police told the group they couldn't enter the city. Trenton mill owners didn't want any trouble. But Mother Jones invited the policemen to stay for lunch. The children gathered around the cooking pot with their tin plates and cups. The policemen smiled, talked kindly to them, then allowed them to cross the bridge into Trenton. There Mother Jones spoke to a crowd of five thousand people. That night, the policemen's wives took the children into their homes, fed them, and packed them lunches for the next day's march.

By now, many of the children were growing weak. More returned home. Some adults on the march grumbled that Mother Jones just wanted people to notice *her.* They complained to reporters that Mother Jones often stayed in hotels while the marchers camped in hot, soggy tents filled with whining mosquitoes. Sometimes Mother Jones did stay in hotels, because she went ahead of the marchers to arrange for lodging and food in upcoming towns and to get publicity for the march.

As the remaining marchers pushed on to Princeton, New Jersey, a thunderstorm struck. Mother Jones and her army camped on the grounds of former President Grover Cleveland's estate. The Clevelands were away, and the caretaker let Mother Jones use the big, cool barn for a dormitory.

Mother Jones got permission from the mayor of Princeton to speak opposite the campus of Princeton University. Her topic: higher education. She spoke to a large crowd of professors, students, and residents. Pointing to one ten-year-old boy, James Ashworth, she said, "Here's a textbook on economics." The boy's body was stooped from carrying seventy-five-pound bundles of yarn. "He gets three dollars a week and his sister, who is fourteen, gets six dollars. They work in a carpet factory ten hours a day while the children of the rich are getting their higher education." Her piercing glance swept over the students in the crowd.

Mother Jones talked about children who could not read or write because they spent ten hours a day in Pennsylvania's silk mills. Those who hired these child workers used "the

Mother Jones leading a protest march in 1903. The march of the mill children also drew crowds.

At Coney Island, the mill children had a rare day of laughing and playing.

hands and feet of little children so they might buy automobiles for their wives and police dogs for their daughters to talk French to." She accused the mill owners of taking "babies almost from the cradle."

The next night, the marchers slept on the banks of the Delaware River. In every town, Mother Jones drew on what she did best—speaking—to gather support for her cause. One reporter wrote, "Mother Jones makes other speakers sound like tin cans."

Battling heat, rain, and swarms of mosquitoes at night, the marchers arrived in Elizabeth. Socialist party members helped house and feed the weary adults and children. The next morning, two businessmen gave Mother Jones her first car ride. She was delighted with this new "contraption."

On July 15, Mother Jones wrote a letter to President Roosevelt. She told him how these poor mill children lived, appealed to him as a father, and asked him to meet with her and the children. President Roosevelt did not answer Mother Jones's letter. Instead, he assigned secret service officers to watch her. They thought she might be a threat to the president. That made her furious.

On July 24, after more than two weeks on the road, the marchers reached New York City. By now, just twenty marchers remained. One of them was Eddie Dunphy, a child whose job was to sit on a high stool eleven hours a day handing thread to another worker. For this he was paid three dollars a week. Mother Jones talked about Eddie and about Gussie Rangnew, a child who packed stockings in a factory. She too worked eleven hours a day for pennies.

At one meeting, a crowd of thirty thousand gathered. "We are quietly marching toward the president's home," she told the people. "I believe he can do something for these children, although the press declares he cannot."

One man wanted the children to have some fun while they were in New York City. Frank Bostick owned the wild animal show at Coney Island, an amusement park and resort. He invited the mill children to spend a day at the park. The children swam in the ocean and played along the beach.

When Frank Bostick's wild animal show ended that night, he let Mother Jones speak to the crowd that had attended. To add drama, she had some of the children crawl inside the empty cages. The smells of sawdust and animals hung in the air. But instead of lions and tigers, the cages held children. The children gripped the iron bars and solemnly stared out at the crowd while Mother Jones spoke.

"We want President Roosevelt to hear the wail of the children who never have a chance to go to school, but work eleven and twelve hours a day in the textile mills of Pennsylvania," she said, "who weave the carpets that he and you walk upon; and the lace curtains in your windows, and the clothes of the people."

She continued, "In Georgia where children work day and night in the cotton mills they have just passed a bill to protect song birds. What about the little children from whom all song is gone?" After Mother Jones finished speaking, the crowd sat in stunned silence. In the distance, a lone lion roared.

The grueling walk had taken almost three weeks. Mother Jones had written the president twice with no answer. On July 29, she took three young boys to Sagamore Hill, where the president was staying. But the secret service stopped them at the mansion's gates. The president would not see them.

The group returned to New York City. Discouraged, Mother Jones reported her failure to the newspapers. Most of the marchers decided to return home. She stayed on briefly with the three children. Once more, she wrote President Roosevelt: "The child of today is the man or woman of tomorrow. . . . I have with me three children who have walked one hundred miles. . . . If you decide to see these children, I will bring them before you at any time you may set."

The president's secretary replied that the president felt that child labor was a problem for individual states to solve. "He is a brave guy when he wants to take a gun out and fight other grown people," said Mother Jones in disgust, "but when those children went to him, he could not see them."

In early August, Mother Jones finally took the last three children home. Soon after, the textile workers gave up and ended their strike. Adults and children went back to work, their working conditions unchanged.

According to Mother Jones, Theodore Roosevelt was a "brave guy" when he could bully other grown-ups. But he didn't have the courage to face the mill children.

Though she had not met with the president, Mother Jones had drawn the attention of the nation to the problem of child labor. She became even more of a national figure. Within a few years, Pennsylvania, New York, New Jersey, and other states did pass tougher child labor laws. The federal government finally passed a child labor law (part of the Fair Labor Standards Act) in 1938—thirty-five years after the march of the mill children.

The United Mine Workers of America was determined to unionize miners in Colorado.

TEN

Mad Dogs in Colorado

1903–1904

After the march of the mill children, Mother Jones visited her friend Eugene Debs in Indiana. Debs planned to run for president in 1904. She rested briefly, but soon she dashed off on a new mission. United Mine Workers president John Mitchell sent Mother Jones to Colorado, a state filled with towering mountains and rich in gold and coal. Conditions were so bad in Colorado's mines that its miners already had a long history of strikes. Mother Jones called these miners "slaves of the dismal caves." Often working by candlelight, they toiled in shafts five hundred to eight hundred feet deep.

The state's eleven thousand miners were divided into two distinct groups. Many of those in the northern fields, near Boulder, belonged to a union. In the more productive southern fields, few miners belonged. Many of the miners in the southern fields had recently come from other countries—Austria, Yugoslavia, Italy, Greece, and Mexico—and spoke limited English.

Mother Jones went to southern Colorado to see for herself how things were. She slipped quietly into the small town of Trinidad on October 26, 1903, and hurried along the dirt streets to the hotel, where she registered as "M. Jones" of Chicago. A few days later she left the hotel disguised as a peddler, wearing an old calico dress and a sunbonnet. In a bag, she carried pins and needles, knives and forks, swatches of fabric, and other supplies to sell.

Mother Jones headed for the coal camps of the Colorado Fuel and Iron Company (CFI). Owned by the wealthy Rockefeller family, CFI was the most powerful coal company in Colorado. It produced nearly half of the coal dug in the state.

Scattered over six hundred square miles, the company's mines were nestled in low mountains and meadows and connected by winding roads. Mother Jones traveled from camp to camp, sometimes staying overnight with mining families. The filth and misery of the camps contrasted sharply with the beauty of Colorado's golden aspen trees against the bright blue sky.

As in other mining states, the company controlled everything on its property. Sometimes several families shared one-room shacks with dirt floors, leaky roofs, and broken windows. Soot belching from the mine's coke ovens choked out any plant life. Piles of tailings—mining residue—loomed nearby. Railroad tracks ran right by the rows of shacks. But if a family complained about their living conditions, the company threw them out.

The hated company guards held the immigrant miners in line with machine guns and rifles. Paid in scrip, miners had no real money of their own. Company agents who weighed the coal often cheated the miners. A miner might dig three tons of coal but only get credit for one.

Mother Jones decided Colorado's miners had good reasons to revolt. She urged John Mitchell to call a strike—one

Many miners in southern Colorado were recent immigrants.

that would include all its coal miners in the state, north and south. Members of another union, the Western Federation of Miners (WFM), were already on strike. The WFM was made up of gold miners, mill workers, and a few coal miners. The two unions had many of the same demands. If the UMW joined the WFM's strike effort, both unions might benefit. John Mitchell hesitated; many in the UMW considered the socialist-leaning WFM too radical. But he finally threw his support behind the idea.

On November 9, 1903, almost ninety-five percent of Colorado's miners did not report for work. The *United Mine Workers Journal* called the walkout "the biggest surprise party in the history of the West." The miners wanted real

A tent colony near Cripple Creek (top). *Mother Jones visited with tent colony families* (below).

money instead of scrip, and they wanted a fair method for weighing the coal. Most important, they demanded that the workday be limited to eight hours.

The CFI immediately threw the miners' families out of their homes. Wagons piled high with dishes, blankets, clothing, and furniture streamed out of the camps. Men carried trunks on their shoulders. Women and children walked beside the wagons. The union was faced with the huge problem of feeding families and finding somewhere for them to live.

Soon the homeless families settled in huge tent colonies off company land. Mother Jones helped bring news, food, and medical supplies to them. In one location she spoke to twenty-five hundred people, encouraging them to keep up the fight. People took off their hats to her. Some shouted, "*Viva* (long live) Mother Jones." Miners had all heard about this "Joan of Arc" of the coal mines. Journalists reported that Mother Jones could stir up a crowd with just a few words and a turn of her head.

Meanwhile, Colorado's entire mining industry had fallen silent. Wintry winds blew. When a gold mine or a mill shut down, people didn't notice the effect right away. But when coal supplies in homes grew dangerously low, Colorado's citizens began to complain. The combined strike effort was taking its toll.

In late November, Mother Jones got a telephone call from Louisville, a town in northern Colorado near Boulder. The crackly voice on the other end of the line said, "For God's sake, Mother, come to us, come to us!" When she wanted to know what the trouble was, the man sputtered, "Don't wait to ask. Don't miss the train!" The northern miners, who had gathered in Louisville, had just been offered a settlement. However, the mine owners had not included the southern miners in the offer. John Mitchell had sent a telegram urging the northern miners to accept.

Mother Jones and William Howells, president of the UMW branch in Trinidad, hurriedly boarded a train for the two-hundred-mile trip to Louisville. At the meeting, Howells spoke first. But the crowd soon called for Mother Jones. She strode vigorously to the front of the stage, her blue eyes crackling with purpose. She began her brief speech calmly, with humor. But she soon got to her main message: unity.

"If you go back to work here and your brothers fall in the south," she told the crowd, "you will be responsible for their defeat. . . . You are all miners fighting a common cause. . . . The iron heel feels the same to all flesh." She urged the miners to stand together, whether they were longtime Americans or recent immigrants, whether they worked in northern or southern Colorado. She added that she wasn't afraid to work with the more radical WFM. A union was a union. "I shall leave a happy woman if I know that you have decided to stand by our suffering brothers in the South," she said. "I will see you again, boys, after I have licked the CF & I."

Her speech had an electrifying effect on the crowd. The northern miners rose and cheered her. They rejected the offer to settle and voted to stand with the southern miners.

John Mitchell was furious with Mother Jones for urging the men to go against his advice. After she returned to southern Colorado, he convinced the northern miners to accept the terms and return to work on November 30, 1903. The next day, northern Colorado mines began producing seven thousand tons of coal a day.

The strike in southern Colorado continued. Bitterly cold winds whipped through the tents on the bleak mountainsides. A foot and a half of snow lay on the ground. People wrapped their feet in gunny sacks; their shoes had long since worn through. Whenever she could, Mother Jones moved among the families, holding meetings and cheering them.

Armed guards patrolled the areas around the mines. Strikers clashed frequently with strikebreakers. In the Cripple Creek area, thirty-three people died in dynamiting and shooting incidents. To restore order, Governor James P. Peabody called out the state militia. He set a 9:00 P.M. curfew. Citizens could no longer gather in crowds or carry guns. Peabody also closed down the Italian language newspaper.

By now, Mother Jones didn't think much of Governor Peabody. "Whenever the masters of the state told the governor to bark," she said of him, "he yelped for them like a mad hound. Whenever they told the military to bite, they bit." One poster showed a United States flag and read "Is Colorado in America?"

In January 1904, the pace of Mother Jones's work caught up with her. She fell ill with pneumonia and spent several weeks in the Trinidad hospital. Worried miners and their families huddled outside in the cold, asking about her.

By March, she was well enough to speak to a group of strikers in Trinidad. But a few days later, on March 26, soldiers came for her and three other organizers. Guards put the group on a train heading south to New Mexico. Mother Jones later boasted, "It took six of Peabody's lap dogs to take me, a woman of sixty-five, and put me on a train to get out of the country." (Careless about details, she was probably closer to seventy-three.) At the border between Colorado and New Mexico, each of the "prisoners" was handed a letter from the governor ordering them never to return.

But Mother Jones never left Colorado. A sympathetic conductor let her board a train headed back north to Denver.

When she got there, she wrote a fiery letter to Governor Peabody. She told him that she'd broken no law. "Mr. Governor," she wrote, "you notified your dogs of war to put me out of the state. . . . I wish to notify you, governor, that you don't own the state. . . . I am right here in the capital. . . four or five blocks from your office. I want to ask you, governor, what in Hell are you going to do about it?"

The governor did nothing. But on April 16, she wrote to John Mitchell, "The next thing the Colorado Canobol [cannibal] will do will be to kill me. That's all they have left undone."

Mother Jones *had* made enemies. Stories in the Denver paper *Polly Pry* called Mother Jones power hungry, "an old hag," and a "vulgar, heartless creature with a fiery temper and a cold-blooded brutality." The oddest charge claimed that in her younger years, Mother Jones had run a house of prostitution. Mother Jones thought this charge harked back to the time she had befriended a Chicago prostitute. She ignored the unlikely story, but it continued to crop up.

In October 1904, the miners in southern Colorado finally gave up and went back to work. The coal companies had spent over a million dollars fighting the strike, the union half that. Some six thousand strikers were blacklisted—no company would hire them back. The United Mine Workers lost members. So did the Western Federation of Miners. Conditions in the southern fields improved very little, and the coal companies went back to business as usual.

The friendship between Mother Jones and John Mitchell was never the same. She blamed him for abandoning the miners in southern Colorado. To her, Mitchell was too willing to compromise, and his lifestyle was too lavish. Shortly after the Colorado strike, she resigned from the UMW. She made it

Mother Jones scolded Governor James P. Peabody when he tried to evict her from Colorado. "You don't own the state," she said. She scolded miners, too, but they felt her fierce loyalty. Poet Carl Sandburg wrote that a young miner in jail "had no mother but Mother Jones."

clear that she would go wherever she could do the most good—even to other unions.

People have wondered what it was that drew miners to Mother Jones. Perhaps it was the way she defended her "boys," whether they were Polish, Irish, Italian, or any other nationality or race. To Mother Jones, miners were miners, no matter what their race or nationality, no matter whether they were union or nonunion. She said of the miners in the wretched camps of CFI, "No more loyal, courageous men could be found than those southern miners, scornfully referred to. . . as 'foreigners.' Italians and Mexicans endured to the end. They were defeated on the industrial field but theirs was the victory of the spirit."

Mother Jones once told a trapper boy, "I would rather be shot fighting for you than live in any palace in America."

ELEVEN

The Most Dangerous Woman in America

1905–1914

After Colorado, Mother Jones plunged into some of her most radical years. She zigzagged across the country, riding a lightning bolt of labor unrest. During this period, the Western Federation of Miners and the Socialist Party paid part of her expenses. By 1911, so did the United Mine Workers of America (she went back on the payroll that year).

Coal miners weren't the only workers she helped. There were telegraphers and dressmakers in Chicago. Copper miners in Michigan, Montana, and Arizona. Lead miners in Idaho. Garment makers in New York and Pennsylvania. Iron ore workers in Minnesota. Railroad workers in the Pacific Northwest. She raised money, encouraged strikers, and lobbied for the release of jailed union leaders.

In June 1905, she and other radical socialists founded the Industrial Workers of the World (IWW), a group that tried to bring together several different unions into one. It later clashed violently with government and business. Mother Jones didn't stay with the group very long. She had other,

Mother Jones marched with striking workers in Michigan.

more important fights to fight. With her friend Jane Addams (founder of Chicago's Hull House), she helped defend two Jewish workers who were about to be deported to Russia to face certain death.

Mother Jones's feisty spirit burst forth from the words of her many speeches and letters. Phrases such as "up to my ears," "not a moment to spare," and "hard at work" showed the fast pace of her life. At times she also expressed disappointment, loneliness, even fear. She wrote often to Terence Powderly, calling him "My dear Mr. Powderly," "My dear friend," or "My dear son." (Powderly was nineteen years younger than Mother Jones.) In 1907, she wrote to him: "I am still alive and fighting the common enemy as best I know how."

As the years sped by, Mother Jones's hair turned snow

white, her kindly face more wrinkled. Her voice, still tinged with an Irish accent, grew higher but not harsh. She walked with a slight limp, but she could still hike for miles. When interviewed at age eighty-three, she said, "I have no time to think about getting old; besides I have a lot to accomplish yet."

Mother Jones went back into West Virginia in 1912. Despite the gains made ten years earlier, conditions had grown worse. The battle had to be fought all over again. Several thousand coal miners went on strike. They worked for forty different companies in the Paint Creek and Cabin Creek area, south of the Kanawha River. The companies hired guards to protect the strikebreakers.

When Mother Jones had to, she could be a quick-witted actress. One day she drove a one-horse buggy at the head of a column of striking miners in the Cabin Creek area. They were marching toward an unorganized coal camp. Suddenly, more than fifty mine guards blocked the road ahead. Morning sun glinted on steel, as the guards fingered the triggers of their machine guns. Mother Jones climbed down and walked calmly up to one of them. Peering over her spectacles, she clamped her hand over the muzzle of his gun.

"Listen, you," she snapped. "Up there in the mountain I have five hundred miners. They are marching armed to the meeting I am going to address. If you start the shooting, they will finish the game." The guards let the strikers pass. Later, Mother Jones admitted there were no miners in the hills. "I realized we were up against it, and something had to be done to save the lives of these poor wretches," she said, "so I pulled the dramatic stuff on them thugs." She told this story often, recalling how the mine guards "shook in their boots."

As much as she was feared and hated by company bosses, Mother Jones was loved by miners. Fred Mooney, a

UMW official who worked with her in West Virginia, said, "The miners loved, worshipped and adored her. . . . There was no night too dark, no danger too great for her to face, if in her judgment 'her boys' needed her."

And yet she scolded them—as only a mother could. She sometimes called them cowards to let themselves be robbed by the mine owners. Telling them to read and educate themselves, she urged, "Don't drink. Go home and be good boys."

The West Virginia strike grew more and more violent, with random shootings, protest marches, and arrests of the strikers. Coal companies hired mine guards from the Baldwin-Felts Detective Agency. Some of these guards attacked tent colonies from trains mounted with machine guns. Mother Jones urged the miners to arm themselves against the "bloodhounds." She called Governor William Glasscock a "dirty coward." Even though she was against violence, she warned Glasscock about violence in the hills unless he got rid of the mine guards. Finally, the governor ordered the area placed under military control.

On February 12, 1913, Mother Jones and a group of miners went to Charleston to talk to him. She was immediately arrested. She was charged with conspiring to commit murder, stealing a machine gun, and attempting to blow up a train. She hadn't done any of those things, but authorities put her in jail anyway. Part of that time she spent in a shack under military guard, with only a straw tick for a bed. She suffered from headaches and pneumonia.

While in jail, she wrote letters but wasn't allowed to mail them. But she talked the guards into helping her. After hiding letters in a hole in the floor covered by a rug, she gave a signal. The guards crawled under the floor to get them. She gave her location as the "Military Bastille." "God

When a West Virginia strike grew violent, the state's governor called in the state militia (above). Mine guards often used scare tactics to discourage strikers, as the newspaper (below) reported.

"MOTHER" JONES TALKS TO MINERS ON CABIN CREEK, AND STRIKE WILL FOLLOW

OBNOXIOUS GUARDS FROM PAINT CREEK WERE TRANSFERRED TO CABIN CREEK— TROUBLE THERE SO ON FOLLOWED—BOOMER TROUBLES ARE PRACTICALLY SETTLED— 6,000 MEN ARE STILL ON STRIKE

spare me the heart to fight them. . . . I'll fight the pirates," she wrote Terence Powderly.

Meanwhile, Congress was looking into the strike and the miners' demands. Mother Jones sent a telegram to Washington, D.C. Prolabor Senator John Kern of Indiana read it before the Senate. "From out the military prison walls of Pratt, West Virginia, where I have walked over my eighty-fourth milestone in history, I send you groans and tears and heartaches of men, women, and children. . . . I plead with you for the honor of this nation to push that investigation, and the children yet unborn will rise and call you blessed." The telegram caused a stir in Congress and in the papers.

Governor Glasscock finally released Mother Jones, offering no explanation for her eighty-five days in jail. The mine war, which had dragged on for fourteen months, ended. Nearly thirty thousand shots had been fired, leaving fifty people dead. Union membership had grown, but the miners had won only limited gains. The fight for miners' rights in West Virginia was far from over.

Mother Jones left West Virginia in the spring of 1913. That fall, she headed for another familiar trouble spot—Colorado. She returned to Trinidad, where miners had been defeated nine years before. She worked with UMW officials John Lawson and Edward Doyle. Both became trusted friends.

Little had changed in southern Colorado since Mother Jones had last been there. Families still lived in cramped, filthy conditions. The accident rate for Colorado mines was twice the national average. The CFI company had refused to meet with the miners, who were on the verge of joining a strike by miners in the north.

Mother Jones fired up miners at a UMW convention in Trinidad, saying, "Rise up and strike. If you are too cowardly to fight for your rights, there are enough women in this country to come and beat hell out of you. If it is slavery or strike, I say strike till the last one of you drop in your graves."

She warned miners not to be afraid of the heavily armed Baldwin-Felts thugs hired as mine guards. "Don't be afraid boys; fear is the greatest curse we have. I never was anywhere yet that I feared anybody. I do what I think is right and when I die I will render an account of it."

On September 23, 1913, some nine thousand miners in southern Colorado went on strike. Once again families left their company-owned houses and trudged through rain and mud to tent colonies in the strike area. Baldwin-Felts guards hunkered down in trenches near the colonies with searchlights and machine guns. They cruised the area in an armored car called the "Death Special." The miners gathered what weapons they could, but they were no match for the guards.

Guards cruised around tent colonies in the "Death Special." The armored car could shoot four hundred times a minute.

Mother Jones marched a ragtag group through the streets of Trinidad to confront Governor Elias Ammons.

Then Colorado's governor, Elias Ammons, came to Trinidad. Mother Jones rounded up a huge crowd of shabbily dressed women and children and went to see him. With a brass band leading the way, she marched the group into the hotel where Governor Ammons was staying. The marchers carried signs that read "We Represent CFI Slaves." Mother Jones pounded on the door of the governor's room. "Unlock that door and come out here!..." she shouted. "These women aren't going to bite you."

The governor stayed inside. He later ordered the state militia, led by General John Chase, into the strike area. Chase was a man so brutally violent that Mother Jones said, "His veins run with ice water."

By now, Mother Jones knew she was in danger. She wrote Terence Powderly, "They are sending me all sorts of threats here. They have my skull drawn on a picture and two cross sticks underneath my jaw to tell me that if I do not quit they are going to get me."

Her suspicions were correct. In early January 1914, General Chase arrested her in Trinidad. He put her on a train going north to Denver and ordered her not to return to southern Colorado. In Denver, Mother Jones bought five hundred dollars' worth of shoes for miners' families. Then she slipped past the detectives guarding her hotel room and headed south, arriving back in Trinidad on January 12.

Calling her a "witch," General Chase arrested her again. This time he used a hospital in Trinidad as a jail, holding her there under armed guard. She was not allowed visitors, exercise, or newspapers. When she became ill, Chase even refused to allow Mother Jones to see a doctor.

Outside the hospital, hundreds of women and children marched in protest. Their banners read "God Bless Mother

When Mother Jones was held prisoner in a hospital, protesters carried banners reading "God Bless Mother Jones."

Jones," "We're for Mother Jones," and "Mother Jones Has Not Done Anything That We Would Not Do."

General Chase ordered his soldiers: "Ride down the women." His men dug their spurs into their horses and attacked the protesters, slashing at them with sabers. One woman almost lost an ear. Another's forehead was cut. A soldier smashed his fist into a small child's face.

Despite the violence, public outcry continued. After nine weeks, Chase released Mother Jones. Again she was banished from southern Colorado, but again she returned. And again, General Chase immediately arrested her. The young soldier making the arrest said, "Will you take my arm, madam?"

Mother Jones snapped back, "No, I won't. You take my suitcase." This time, Mother Jones spent twenty-six days in a damp basement jail cell in Walsenburg, Colorado. A single light bulb hung overhead. She could not send or receive letters or see the daily newspaper.

"It was cold, it was a horrible place, and they thought it would sicken me, but I concluded to stay in that cellar and fight them out," she said. "I had sewer rats that long every night to fight, and all I had was a beer bottle; I would get one

A newspaper in Denver reported that Mother Jones told the governor "what's what."

rat and another would run across the cellar at me. I fought the rats inside and out just alike."

Outside, blue mountain columbine and red Indian paint-brush had begun to bud on the hillsides. "I watched people's feet from my cellar window," said Mother Jones, who had nothing else to do, "miners' feet in old shoes; soldiers' feet, well shod in government leather; the shoes of women with the heels run down; the dilapidated shoes of children; bare-footed boys. The children would scrooch down and wave to me, but the soldiers shooed them off."

One of her jailers, "a man with a heart," brought her extra food. Once in a while, she slipped the "nice young men" in the militia some change. One of them apparently helped her smuggle out a letter. Published in a Denver newspaper, the letter said, "Of course I long to be out of jail. To be shut off from the sunlight is not pleasant." But jail didn't awe her. "I shall stand firm," she said.

Fewer laws protected the rights of citizens in 1914 than today. No formal charges had ever been filed against Mother Jones, yet she remained in jail. In early April, she was sud-denly released—no explanation given.

The weeks in jail and struggles during the strike had worn Mother Jones down. Despite her exhaustion, she left immediately for Washington, D.C., to testify before a con-gressional committee studying the Colorado mine wars.

A few days later, tragic events drew her back to southern Colorado. Ludlow was one of the tent colonies in the strike area. Half of its one thousand residents were women and chil-dren. Families of many different nationalities lived in two hundred tents. As tensions in the area grew, mine guards, pit bosses, and state militia guarded Ludlow.

On April 20, 1914, soldiers suddenly attacked the tent

colony. They fired machine guns, lobbed bombs, and set tents on fire with oil-soaked torches. Ludlow burned to the ground. Thirty-two people died when they were shot or burned in the fire. A group of two women and their eleven small children had dug themselves into a pit under an iron cot inside their tent to hide; they died as the tent burned and collapsed around them.

The Ludlow massacre made headlines all over the country. Angry miners went on a ten-day rampage, destroying company buildings. President Woodrow Wilson sent in federal troops to replace the state militia.

Mother Jones immediately went to work raising money for the Ludlow families and telling their story. She also asked John D. Rockefeller Jr. to go to southern Colorado and see what was really going on in his mining camps. Rockefeller refused, but he did meet with Mother Jones. Even though she

Soldiers surrounding Ludlow opened fire on April 20, 1914.

When a group of women and children hid in this pit, they were burned to death.

called him a "high class burglar," the two took a few steps toward making peace.

President Wilson proposed a three-year plan for industrial peace in Colorado—an effort that won Mother Jones's lasting respect. The plan would have given miners an eighthour day and higher wages. But mine owners turned down the plan. The strike ended in defeat on December 7, 1914.

The Colorado coal strike of 1913–1914 was one of the most violent and demanding strikes Mother Jones took part in. Afterward, she gave a simple explanation for why the miners lost. "They had only the constitution," she said. "The other side had bayonets. In the end, the bayonets always win."

Soldiers burned Ludlow to the ground during the Colorado coal strike of 1913–1914. Thirty-two people died.

This 1914 sketch by Maurice Becker is in the collection of the Smithsonian Institution in Washington, D.C.

TWELVE

"Women Are Fighters"
1910–1915

People thought of Mother Jones as a protector of children and the miners' angel. But she also believed strongly in the power of women. "It is the women who decide the fate of a nation," she said. Even though most of her close friends were men, she often criticized men for not being as strong as women.

"Women are fighters," she said in a speech. She said women were "the inner life of the human race, every drop of their blood precious." She believed educating women could only help the cause of labor. At a time when the idea of "sisterhood" was new, Mother Jones said, "As soon as every woman grasps the idea that every other woman is her sister, then we will begin to better conditions."

Mother Jones drew poor women to her like a magnet. Once she gathered a crowd of older women, young girls, and mothers with babies in a Pennsylvania barn. By the light of a flickering lantern, she stepped up on a box. Then she flung her arms wide and shouted, "Sisters!"

She began to speak in a low, friendly voice, as if she were

talking over the fence to the women. Her language was softer and not as filled with swear words as it sometimes was with men. She talked about the march the women would make to a neighboring town to convince the miners there to join a strike. Her listeners drew near and leaned their elbows on her speaking box.

Gradually her words grew more intense. Tears ran down the women's cheeks as Mother Jones told a particularly sad story about a mining family. Then she broke the mood with a wisecrack. The women burst into laughter. Soon her words rang from the rafters. Women like these, whose lives held many hardships and few joys, had always been close to Mother Jones's heart.

One of her most successful efforts with women had come in 1910 when she had organized the female workers in the beer factories of Milwaukee, Wisconsin. At that time, Mother Jones was eighty. Some six to seven hundred young girls and women worked in the breweries. Many of them had come recently to the United States, were uneducated, and spoke little English. Others were young American-born women without families, struggling to survive on their own.

Most of the women were bottle washers. The rooms where they scrubbed the beer bottles were damp, the floors drenched with soapy, dirty water. As a result, the women usually worked in soaking wet clothing. Many suffered from aching joints and lung diseases.

"The poor girls slave on all day in the vile smell of sour beer," observed Mother Jones, "lifting cases of empty and full bottles weighing from 100 to 150 pounds, in their wet shoes and rags."

At the end of a long day, bottle washers often cleaned the factory lunchrooms and did other odd jobs for no extra

Bottle washers in Milwaukee demanded a union.

pay. Foremen controlled the women closely, even watching how much time they spent in the bathroom.

Bottle washers earned seventy-five to eighty cents a day. This was barely enough money for food and lodging, and seldom enough for the luxury of a streetcar ride. During the bitterly cold winters, many women trudged home in their wet clothes and shoes through deep, snowy drifts to the shacks where they lived.

From January to March, Mother Jones studied the breweries, asking the women questions and listening to their sad tales. Then she went to see the owner of the Blatz Brewery. She told him the women needed a union. He said they got married and moved away anyway; they didn't need to be organized. When members of the brewers' association refused to let Mother Jones inspect their factories, she threatened to talk to lawmakers in Madison, the capital of Wisconsin.

She did something even better. She went to the United Mine Workers convention in Cincinnati, Ohio, and asked the men to help her. Most of the beer drunk in mining camps came from Milwaukee. She asked the miners not to buy Milwaukee beer. Then she said they'd give the brewers "the damnedest fight they have ever had." She went on, "One of the boys said I was looking well. Of course I am. There is going to be a racket and I am going to be in it! When I get a lick at them, it makes me young again."

Mother Jones's scheme was clever. If over five hundred thousand miners refused to drink beer brewed in Milwaukee, the brewery owners would quickly feel the effects. Under the threat of the boycott, the brewery owners gave in. The bottle washers got their union. The women gained wage increases and better working conditions.

Most of the women Mother Jones met had to work in mills, factories, and breweries because they needed money. Ideally, she felt, women belonged at home raising their children. If wages improved for husbands, wives wouldn't have to work outside the home.

As mothers, women could solve many of the problems of the world, Mother Jones believed. When World War I broke out in 1914, Mother Jones said that women could stop that war. In fact, they could stop all wars by training their children to play in peaceful ways. "Any woman who buys a toy gun or pistol for her child ought to be put in a sanitarium," she said.

One prickly issue in Mother Jones's life was her opposition to suffrage—voting rights for women. Before 1920, only men could vote in national elections. Mother Jones deeply distrusted politics, so she didn't think women should get involved. This view pitted her against suffragists such as Susan B. Anthony, Elizabeth Cady Stanton, Lucy Stone, and others. They fought hard for women's right to vote in the late nineteenth and early twentieth centuries.

"I have never had a vote," said Mother Jones, "and I have raised hell all over this country! You don't need a vote to raise hell! You need convictions and a voice! . . . I have been up against armed mercenaries, but this old woman, without a vote, and with nothing but a hat pin has scared them."

In some states, such as Colorado, women could vote in state elections. To Mother Jones, that didn't seem to help matters much. "The women of Colorado have had the vote for two generations and the working men and women are in slavery," she said.

Mother Jones believed in putting first things first. She felt poor women needed food, shelter, and clothing much more than they needed the right to vote. She may have seen the right to vote as a rich woman's issue, not a working class cause. She thought the only battle worth fighting was the one for making all classes of people equal. She didn't think women needed a vote to fight that fight.

Yet in some of her speeches and writings, she hinted at a different view. She once suggested that Congress needed a woman to shake it up. In 1915, she spoke to Congress about the march of the mill children. She poked fun at Theodore Roosevelt, who had been president then. "He had a lot of

Mother Jones had no time for the latest fashions—such as the feathered hat worn by this woman.

secret service men watching an old woman and an army of children," she said. "You fellows do elect wonderful presidents. The best thing you can do is to put a woman in the next time."

Despite Mother Jones's tough image, people often commented on her ladylike appearance. One reporter described her as "wonderful in her black silk, her carefully dressed, silvery hair, her silk stockings and neat pumps." She even carried a powder puff.

Yet this costume was just a uniform. She said, "A lady is a female whose skull is adorned with four feet of feathers. A woman is a female whose skull is full of gray matter." She called fashionable women "bluffs" and "poor, ignorant geese." She criticized wealthy women with their maids and social clubs.

"No matter what your fight, don't be ladylike!" she said. "God almighty made women and the Rockefeller gang of thieves made the ladies."

Mother Jones brought shoes to a mother and children in Ludlow. Mother Jones believed in putting first things first. She fought for essentials for poor women and their families.

Terence Powderly (left) *and Mother Jones* (right) *were lifelong friends.*

THIRTEEN

"An Old War Horse Wearing Down"

1916–1930

Many American citizens were beginning to think of people in the labor movement as dangerous radicals. Some called Mother Jones a Bolshevik (Bolsheviks were socialist radicals in the Russian revolution). She even called herself a Bolshevik once. But Mother Jones insisted that she never "played politics." "I have been a Socialist for twenty-nine years and I would hammer a Socialist if he is a crazy lunatic just the same as anyone else," she said.

The United States was not the only country in which Mother Jones was a labor hero. A revolution in Mexico from 1908 to 1910 had forced rebel leaders to flee to the United States. The rebels had been jailed in California on false charges of murder, robbery, and violating international law.

Mother Jones had raised money for the rebels and had protested their unfair treatment. She had asked then-President Taft to pardon them. Taft had told her, "Now, Mother, the trouble lies here: if I put the pardoning power in your hands, there would be no one left in the jails."

She had answered, "I'm not so sure of that, Mr. President. . . . A lot of those who are in would be out, but a lot of those who are out would be in." President Taft had chuckled; later he had pardoned the Mexican prisoners. Because of what she had done for the rebels, Mother Jones became known as *Madre Juanita* in Mexico.

In January 1921, the Mexican government invited Mother Jones, now ninety-one, to speak at an international conference in Mexico City. Leaders at this conference hoped to promote better understanding among the workers of the United States, Mexico, and other countries in Central America. Fred Mooney, the UMW friend Mother Jones had worked with in West Virginia, went with her.

About forty miles from Mexico City, cheering workers from a jewelry factory blocked the path of their train, forcing it to stop. Carrying red carnations and blue violets, the workers jumped on board and piled the flowers around Mother Jones until only her head and shoulders showed. "Welcome to Mexico, *Madre Juanita*," they shouted.

In Mexico City, two thousand workers cheered wildly for Mother Jones. The government of Mexico loaned her a car and driver and a villa to stay in and paid all of her expenses. The warm reception in Mexico surprised Mother Jones. It didn't seem to matter that some of her listeners could not understand her language.

She traveled to Mexico again in April. Before she left, Terence Powderly warned her to watch her health. "There is only one Mother Jones," he wrote. While in Mexico, she visited the coal mines of Coahuila. "The life of the miner is the same wherever coal is dug," she observed. The president of Mexico later sent her five hundred dollars in gold with a note expressing his country's devotion, love, and respect.

Mother Jones returned from Mexico exhausted. She was also suffering from rheumatism, which made her joints stiff and swollen. Ever since her days in jail, she'd had sudden, painful attacks of the disease. Mother Jones never fussed much about her health. But when she was in pain, she often went to stay with friends in California.

In 1922, she went to Terence Powderly's Washington, D.C., home to rest. For many years, the extra room in his comfortable home had been open to her whenever she wanted it. By now Powderly and his wife Emma were paying for most of Mother Jones's medical and other expenses. They considered her part of their family.

Mother Jones had always said very little about her own families—both the one she grew up with and the one she lost to yellow fever. In 1923, her younger brother, William Harris, died. The well-known dean of a Catholic archdiocese in Canada, he was also a writer and a historian. The two seem to have had no contact as adults. But Mother Jones kept a magazine clipping telling of his death with her other papers.

Mother Jones was deeply saddened when Terence Powderly died on June 24, 1924. She spent most of that year writing her autobiography, which was published in 1925 by the Charles H. Kerr Company of Chicago. The text of the autobiography is peppery and straightforward. The events in her life unfold at a dizzying speed. As usual, she placed great importance on telling a good story. She paid less attention to including correct dates, places, and other facts.

She still spent winter with friends in California and spring and early summer with Emma Powderly in Washington, D.C. On her way across the country, she often stayed with the John Walker family in Springfield, Illinois. Walker was like a grandson to her. She wrote him weekly in her later years.

In 1927, at age ninety-seven, she spent four weeks in a Washington hospital with severe rheumatism and pneumonia. Her body had grown frail, and she was gradually losing her sight and her hearing. Her doctors suggested she take a little whiskey. Prohibition—a law banning alcoholic drinks—was in force by then, but doctors could prescribe liquor as a medicine. "I don't like the stuff," she explained, "but I have to take it."

For the next two years she lived with Emma Powderly. Emma eventually found caring for Mother Jones too much of a burden. So Mother Jones went to stay with Walter and Lillian Burgess, a retired miner and his wife who lived on a farm outside Washington. In letters Mother Jones wrote to friends, she said she hoped to live to be a hundred.

But her health grew worse. Many days she didn't get out of bed. Other times she was lively and talkative and got dressed and sat in a rocking chair by the window. She liked seeing the sunshine, trees, and flowers. The peaceful sounds of the farm soothed her—birds singing, cowbells jangling, and roosters scrawking. About this time, she told a reporter that she was "just an old war horse . . . ready for a battle . . . but too worn out to move."

Mother Jones had been bedridden for several months when she reached her hundredth birthday on May 1, 1930. She put on her best black silk dress, and friends carried her outside. Waiting for her there was a huge, five-layer cake with one hundred candles. Though she was thin, her eyes were bright, her cheeks pink with excitement. That day she received some 325 guests in what turned out to be a lively party.

Reporters and photographers with movie cameras recorded the event. Mother Jones was excited to become part of the "newfangled talkies"—motion pictures with

Mother Jones at her hundredth birthday party

sound. But when the "movietone" man tried to tell her how to speak on camera, she snapped, "What the hell do you know about it? I was making speeches before you were born!"

Then she looked into the camera, took a drink of water, and began to speak on a number of topics. Sounding as if she wanted to fling a torch to women who would come after her, she said, "Women can do so much if they only realize their power. . . . Nobody wants a lady. They want women. Ladies are parlor parasites."

That day, Mother Jones was overwhelmed by all the people who sent flowers, presents, and letters. John D. Rockefeller Jr. sent a telegram with his "heartiest congratulations." She still felt Rockefeller didn't understand the working class.

But he read the Bible, she'd heard, so he probably had a Christian heart.

"He's a damn good sport," she said. "I've licked him many times, but now we've made peace. . . . This telegram rather squares things." She sent a telegram back saying his message was a highlight of her day.

A few months after her birthday, Mother Jones gave her last interview. The reporter found Mother Jones "primped up," as she liked to be for guests. Her white-haired head rested against big, soft pillows; her thin, veined hand reached out in welcome. The reporter had no trouble getting her to talk about her life. "We've won out!" Mother Jones said, her eyes blazing, when she talked about the child labor laws that had been passed in many states.

"I haven't been very discreet in my language," she said of her swearing. "You've got to talk a language people can understand. The public is the sleepiest damn bunch you ever saw. You've got to wake them up! Then you get action."

By now, John L. Lewis had become president of the United Mine Workers. Mother Jones didn't like Lewis. She thought of him as a heavy-handed powerbroker who used lies and force to get what he wanted. In September 1930, Mother Jones gave John Walker a thousand dollars to use in an effort to oust Lewis.

In the following weeks, she began to fade in and out of consciousness. During clear moments, she asked to see Walker and other friends. Soon she was unable to consume anything but brandy. On Sunday, November 30, 1930, at 11:55 P.M., Mother Jones did something she had never done before—she slipped quietly away.

At her funeral in Washington, D.C., the church was packed with union leaders, friends, politicians, and strangers.

A small group of unemployed workers in tattered clothing sat near the back of the church. Workers from eight different trades acted as pallbearers.

Mother Jones had asked to be buried in Mount Olive, Illinois, in the miners' cemetery dedicated to those who died in the Virden massacre of 1898. She wanted to "sleep under the clay with those brave boys." In Mount Olive, thousands of coal miners and their families filed past her open casket. She was dressed in lavender, an unusually bright color for her.

Many newspaper articles, songs, and poems were written about Mother Jones when she died. Six years after her death, a miners' group erected a huge granite monument to her at the Mount Olive cemetery. A progressive magazine

In Mount Olive, Illinois, thousands paid their respects when Mother Jones died.

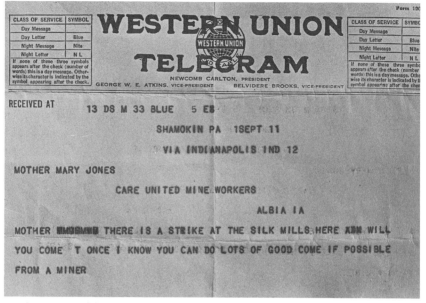

A miner cabled Mother Jones, asking for her help.

was later named after her. In 1992 she was inducted into the Department of Labor Hall of Fame in Washington, D.C. Visitors can learn more about her there.

Mother Jones's warmth, humor, and spirit made her a legendary folk hero, one of the most beloved women in America. Among her many friends and admirers were some of the United States's most powerful citizens and some of its poorest people. Yet because of her unyielding views, she had often stood alone on issues. Many of her efforts failed. But she never lost her focus—freedom for the working class.

Throughout her life, Mother Jones always chose to go "wherever the fight was the fiercest." One of her last wishes was that she could "live another hundred years in order to fight to the end that there would be no more machine guns and no more sobbing of little children."

The world today is mourning
The death of Mother Jones;
Grief and sorrow hover
Over the miners' homes;
This grand old champion of labor
Has gone to a better land,
But the hard-working miners,
They miss her guiding hand.

Through the hills and over the valleys,
In every mining town,
Mother Jones was ready to help them—
She never turned them down.
In front with the striking miners
She always could be found,
She fought for right and justice,
She took a noble stand.

With a spirit strong and fearless
She hated that which was wrong;
She never gave up fighting,
Until her breath was gone.
May the workers all get together
To carry out her plan,
And bring back better conditions
To every laboring man.
—Anonymous

Miners erected this granite
monument to Mother Jones in
Mount Olive, Illinois.

Sources

p. 10   Mary Harris Jones, *The Autobiography of Mother Jones* (1925; reprint, Chicago: Charles H. Kerr & Co., 1972), 51.

p. 11   Ibid., 145.

p. 12   Ibid., 147.

p. 13   Dale Fetherling, *Mother Jones: The Miners' Angel* (Carbondale and Edwardsville: Southern Illinois University Press, 1974), 10.

p. 15   Ibid., 1.

p. 18   Jones, *Autobiography,* 11.

p. 25   Linda S. Atkinson, *Mother Jones: The Most Dangerous Woman in America* (New York: Crown Publishers, 1978), 34.

p. 25–26   Jones, *Autobiography,* 12.

p. 28   Ibid., 13.

p. 31   Edward M. Steel, *The Speeches and Writings of Mother Jones* (Pittsburgh: University of Pittsburgh Press, 1988), xv.

p. 32   Ibid., xiii.

pp. 37–38   Jones, *Autobiography,* 15.

p. 39   Ibid., 17.

p. 41   Ibid.

p. 44   Ibid., 24.

p. 45   Ibid., 26.

p. 46   Ibid., 115–116.

p. 47   Ibid., 118.

pp. 48   Philip S. Foner, ed., *Mother Jones Speaks: Collected Writings and Speeches* (New York: Monad Press, 1983), 453.

p. 49   Jones, *Autobiography,* 124.

p. 49   Ibid., 120.

p. 49   Foner, *Mother Jones Speaks,* 454

p. 50   Jones, *Autobiography,* 122.

p. 50   Ibid.

p. 50   Foner, *Mother Jones Speaks,* 454.

p. 51   Ibid., 127.

p. 51   Ibid., 125.

p. 51   *Holy Bible,* King James Version, Mark 10:14.

p. 51   Jones, *Autobiography,* 126.

p. 52   Foner, *Mother Jones Speaks,* pp. 91–93.

p. 53   Jones, *Autobiography,* 125–126.

p. 54   Ibid., 29.

p. 54   Ibid., 114.

p. 54   Edward M. Steel, *The Correspondence of Mother Jones* (Pittsburgh: University of Pittsburgh Press, 1985), 119.

p. 61   Jones, *Autobiography,* 129.

p. 63   Ibid., 31.

p. 64   Ibid., 32.

p. 66   Ibid., 35.

p. 67   Fetherling, *Mother Jones,* 39.

p. 67   Foner, *Mother Jones Speaks,* 39.

pp. 67–68   Jones, *Autobiography,* 36–37.

p. 68   Fetherling, *Mother Jones,* 37

p. 68   Jones, *Autobiography,* 39.

p. 69   Ibid., 91.

p. 69   Ibid., 93.

p. 69   Ibid., 89.

p. 69   Ibid., 36.

p. 69   Ibid., 91.

p. 71   Jones, *Autobiography,* 235.

p. 72   Fetherling, *Mother Jones,* 27.

p. 72   Steel, *Speeches and Writings,* 270.

p. 74   Foner, *Mother Jones Speaks,* 158.

p. 74   Jones, *Autobiography,* 40–41.

p. 74   Fetherling, *Mother Jones,* 29.

p. 74   Steel, *Correspondence,* 20.

p. 75 Ibid.
p. 75 Ibid., 23.
p. 75 Jones, *Autobiography,* 41–42.
p. 75 Steel, *Correspondence,* 21.
pp. 75–76 Ibid.
p. 77 Jones, *Autobiography,* 43–44.
p. 78 Ibid., 49.
p. 78 Ibid., 50.
p. 78 Ibid., 51.
pp. 78–79 Foner, *Mother Jones Speaks,* 88.
p. 80 Ibid., 89.
p. 81 Jones, *Autobiography,* 63.
p. 81 Ibid., 65.
p. 83 Foner, *Mother Jones Speaks,* 38.
p. 84 Jones, *Autobiography,* 71.
p. 84 Ibid., 72.
p. 84 Ibid.
pp. 84–85 Ibid.
p. 85 Foner, *Mother Jones Speaks,* 100–103.
p. 88 Jones, *Autobiography,* 76–77.
p. 89 Ibid., 76.
p. 90 Steel, *Speeches and Writings,* xvi.
p. 90 Atkinson, *Mother Jones,* 127.
p. 91 Fetherling, *Mother Jones,* 54.
pp. 91–92 Jones, *Autobiography,* 80.
p. 92 Steel, *Correspondence,* 46–48.
p. 92 Fetherling, *Mother Jones,* 56.
p. 95 Steel, *Correspondence,* 21.
p. 99 Jones, *Autobiography,* 97.
p. 100 Foner, *Mother Jones Speaks,* 104–107.
p. 101 Jones, *Autobiography,* 94.
p. 101 Atkinson, *Mother Jones,* 146.
p. 101 Foner, *Mother Jones Speaks,* 110.
p. 102 Jones, *Autobiography,* 103.
p. 102 Steel, *Correspondence,* 50.
p. 102 Atkinson, *Mother Jones,* 147.
p. 103 Jones, *Autobiography,* 113.
p. 106 Steel, *Correspondence,* 63.
p. 107 Foner, *Mother Jones Speaks,* 6.
p. 107 Jones, *Autobiography,* 157–159.
p. 107 Ronnie Gilbert, *Ronnie Gilbert on Mother Jones: Face to Face with the Most Dangerous Woman in America* (Berkeley: Conari Press, 1993), 23.
p. 108 Fetherling, *Mother Jones,* 91.
p. 108 Foner, *Mother Jones Speaks,* 193.
p. 108 Steel, *Correspondence,* 108.
p. 110 Jones, *Autobiography,* 165.
pp. 110–111 Fetherling, *Mother Jones,* 114.
p. 111 Foner, Mother Jones Speaks, 226–235.
p. 113 Fetherling, *Mother Jones,* 116.
p. 113 Jones, *Autobiography,* 183.
p. 113 Steel, *Correspondence,* 119.
p. 114 Foner, *Mother Jones Speaks,* 241.
p. 115 Fetherling, *Mother Jones,* 122.
pp. 115–116 Ibid.
p. 116 Jones, *Autobiography,* 185–186.
p. 116 "Mother Jones versus Mr. Rockefeller," *Metropolitan,* July 1914, n.p.
p. 119 Fetherling, *Mother Jones,* 131.
p. 119 Jones, *Autobiography,* 202.
p. 121 Foner, *Mother Jones Speaks,* 468.
p. 121 Ibid., 91-93.
p. 121 Ibid., 26-27.
p. 121 Ibid., 469.
p. 122 Ibid., 465.
p. 124 Steel, *Speeches and Writings,* 40–42.
p. 125 Foner, *Mother Jones Speaks,* 470.
p. 125 Jones, *Autobiography,* 203–204.
p. 125 Ibid., 203.

pp. 125–126 Foner, *Mother Jones Speaks*, 440.

p. 126 Gilbert, *Ronnie Gilbert on Mother Jones*, 17.

p. 127 Atkinson, *Mother Jones*, 193.

p. 127 Foner, *Mother Jones Speaks*, 468-469.

p. 127 Jones, *Autobiography*, 204.

p. 129 Steel, *Speeches and Writings*, 155.

pp. 129–130 Jones, *Autobiography*, 142.

p. 130 Steel, *Correspondence*, 224–225.

p. 130 Jones, *Autobiography*, 239.

p. 132 Fetherling, *Mother Jones*, 200.

p. 132 Ibid., 201.

p. 133 Ibid., 165.

p. 133 Steel, *Correspondence*, 346.

p. 134 Fetherling, *Mother Jones*, 203.

p. 134 Foner, *Mother Jones Speaks*, 534.

p. 134 Ibid., 536.

p. 135 Foner, *Mother Jones Speaks*, 695.

p. 136 Clarence Darrow, foreword to *The Autobiography of Mother Jones*.

p. 136 Fetherling, *Mother Jones*, 215.

p. 137 Foner, *Mother Jones Speaks*, 67–68.

Bibliography

Writings of Mother Jones

Foner, Philip S., ed. *Mother Jones Speaks: Collected Writings and Speeches.* New York: Monad Press, 1983.

Jones, Mary Harris. *The Autobiography of Mother Jones.* Ed. Mary Field Parton. 1925. Reprint, Chicago: Charles H. Kerr & Co. for the Illinois Labor History Society, 1972.

Steel, Edward M., ed. *The Correspondence of Mother Jones.* Pittsburgh: University of Pittsburgh Press, 1985.

———. *The Speeches and Writings of Mother Jones.* Pittsburgh: University of Pittsburgh Press, 1988.

Other Sources

Angle, Paul M. *The Great Chicago Fire.* Chicago: Chicago Historical Society, 1946.

Atkinson, Linda S. *Mother Jones: The Most Dangerous Woman in America.* New York: Crown Publishers, 1978.

Bruce, Robert. *1877: Year of Violence.* Indianapolis and New York: Bobbs-Merrill Co., 1959.

Fetherling, Dale. *Mother Jones: The Miners' Angel.* Carbondale and Edwardsville: Southern Illinois University Press, 1974.

Gilbert, Ronnie. *Ronnie Gilbert on Mother Jones: Face to Face with the Most Dangerous Woman in America.* Berkeley: Conari Press, 1993.

Harriman, Mrs. J. Borden. *From Pinafores to Politics.* New York: Henry Holt & Co., 1923.

Long, Priscilla. *Mother Jones, Woman Organizer.* Cambridge, Mass.: Red Sun Press, 1976.

McGovern, George S., and Leonard F. Guttridge. *The Great Coalfield War.* Boston: Houghton Mifflin Co., 1972.

Papanikolas, Zeese. *Buried Unsung.* Salt Lake City: University of Utah Press, 1982.

Settle, Mary Lee. *The Scapegoat.* New York: Random House, 1980.

Spargo, John. *The Bitter Cry of the Children.* New York: Garret Press, Inc., 1970.

Steel, Edward M. "Mother Jones in the Fairmont Field, 1902." *Journal of American History,* September 1970, pp. 290–307.

Index

Addams, Jane, 106
American Railway Union, 45
Ammons, Governor Elias, 113
Appeal to Reason, 53–54
Arnot, Pennsylvania, 63–68

Baldwin-Felts Detective Agency, 108, 111
Baltimore and Ohio Railroad, 36
blacks, 19, 44, 57, 79–80
bosses. *See* company owners
Bostick, Frank, 91
bottle washers, 122–124
Bouncer, William, 63, 64
breaker boys, 60–61, 71–72, 83
Burgess, Walter and Lillian, 132

capitalism, 53
Chase, General John, 113–115
Chicago-Virden Coal Company, 57
child labor, 28, 47–51, 52, 53, 60–61, 71, 83–93, 134
Civil War, 19–21
Clarksburg Fuel Company, 76
Cleveland, President Grover, 46, 88
coal miners, 43–45, 57; anthracite, 59, 68–69, 78–79, 80; Colorado, 95–103, 110–113, 116–119; West Virginia, 55–56, 71–81, 107–110; women fighting for rights of, 9–12, 56, 64–67, 69, 113
Colorado, 95–102, 110–119
Colorado Fuel and Iron Company (CFI), 96, 99–100, 103, 110, 113
company owners, 9–10, 38, 64, 69, 72, 74, 84, 89, 107–108; fighting strikers, 11, 57, 68, 75
company stores, 44, 47, 57, 69, 72
Congress, 110, 116, 125
cotton mills, 47–49, 53, 92

"Death Special," 111
Debs, Eugene, 45, 47, 54–56, 95
Department of Labor Hall of Fame, 136
Doyle, Edward, 110

Erie Company, 63, 68

Fair Labor Standards Act, 93
Fairmont Coal Company, 76
federal troops, 36–38, 46, 57, 117
financial panics of 1873 and 1876, 32, 35

Glasscock, Governor William, 108, 110
Great Chicago Fire, 28–29
Great Northern Railway, 45
Great Upheaval, 35–38

Haggerty, Thomas, 59, 73, 76, 80
Harris, Mary. *See* Jones, Mother
Harris, William (brother), 18, 131
Hayes, President Rutherford B., 36
Haymarket Square, 41
Howells, William, 100

immigrant workers, 13, 28, 95, 96, 103
Industrial Workers of the World (IWW), 105
iron molders, 19–21, 23, 30
Iron Molders International Union, 20–21, 23, 26, 31

Jackson, Judge John Jay, 78, 80
Jones, George E. (husband), 19–21, 23, 25, 26
Jones, Mother: appearance of, 9, 31, 43, 62, 107, 126–127; autobiography of, 131; birth of, 15; children of, 23, 25; death of, 134, 137; as dressmaker, 18, 27–30, 31, 39; education of, 17–18; health of, 101, 108, 113, 126, 131, 132, 134; in jail, 71, 78, 108–110, 113–116; organizer for Knights of Labor, 30–33; organizer for UMW, 43–45, 57, 59, 62, 69, 71–76, 78, 95, 105, 110, 122; public image of, 13, 43, 69, 88, 102, 121, 136; as socialist, 53–54, 105, 129;

speeches by, 12–13, 18, 31–32, 51, 62, 71, 73–74, 78, 88–90, 100, 106; as teacher, 18–19; views on nationality and race, 79–80, 100, 103; as wife, 19–25

Kern, Senator John, 110
Knights of Labor, 30–33, 39, 43. *See also* United Mine Workers of America (UMW)

labor movement, 13, 32, 38–39, 129
labor unions, 10, 31, 32, 41. *See also* American Railway Union; Iron Molders International Union; Knights of Labor; United Mine Workers of America (UMW); Western Federation of Miners (WFM)
Lawson, John, 110
Lewis, John L., 134
Lincoln, Abraham, 19
Ludlow massacre, 116–117

march of the mill children, 85–93, 125–126
Mexico, 129–131
mills. *See* textile industry
miners. *See* coal miners
Mitchell, John, 63, 67, 69, 74–76, 80–81, 95–97, 100, 102
Mooney, Fred, 107–108, 130
Mount Olive, Illinois, 57, 135

Norton, West Virginia, strike, 44–45, 46

Peabody, Governor James P., 101–102
Pennsylvania, 9–12, 59–69
Pennsylvania Railroad, 35–38
Pinchgut slum, 20, 25
police violence, 37–38, 41
Polly Pry, 102
pound parties, 56
Powderly, Emma, 131–132
Powderly, Terence, 32, 39–40,

106, 110, 113, 130, 131
Pullman Palace Car Company, 45
Pullman strike, 45–46, 54

railroad workers, 35–38, 45–46
Rockefeller, John D., Jr., 96, 117, 119, 133–134
Roosevelt, President Theodore, 80, 85, 90–92, 125–126
rope factories, 49–50

scabs. *See* strikebreakers
scrip, 72, 99
slavery, 19, 21
socialism, 53–54, 97, 105, 129
Socialist Party, 90, 105
state militias, 37–38, 45, 101, 113, 116
strikebreakers, 10, 41, 55, 56, 64–67, 101, 107; black, 57, 79–80
strikes, 33, 39–40; for higher wages, 10, 36, 44–45, 55–57, 63–69, 76–81, 119, 124; for improved working conditions, 10, 21, 31, 44, 69, 81, 107–113, 124; for shorter work hours, 40–41, 76–81, 83, 96–102, 119; violence and, 10, 37–38, 41, 45, 107, 108, 116–117. *See also* Arnot, Pennsylvania; Great Upheaval; Norton, West Virginia, strike; Pullman strike
suffrage, 125

Taft, President William Howard, 129–130
tent colonies, 99, 108, 111, 116–119
textile industry, 47, 50–51, 83–93. *See also* cotton mills; rope factories
trapper boys, 42, 61, 71
Trinidad, Colorado, 100, 101, 110–111, 113–115

United Mine Workers Journal, 97
United Mine Workers of America (UMW): in Colorado, 95–102,

110–113; conventions, 78–80, 124; formation of, 43; membership of, 69, 102; in Pennsylvania, 59, 62–63; presidents of, 63, 74, 134; in West Virginia, 55, 71–81

Virden massacre, 57, 135

Walker, John, 73, 81, 131, 134
West Virginia, 43–45, 55–56, 71–81, 107–110
Western Federation of Miners (WFM), 97, 100, 102, 105
Wilson, President Woodrow, 117, 119
Wilson, William, 59, 74, 75–76
women: fighting for miners'

rights, 9–13, 56, 64–67, 69, 113, 121–122; lives of, 63, 122; power of, 66, 126–127, 133; and suffrage, 125; and unions, 21, 69; working, 122–124
working class: health problems of, 44, 49, 59–61, 84, 122; living conditions of, 20, 28, 35, 44, 47–48, 96, 110; wages of, 20, 35, 38, 49–50, 57, 59–60, 72, 88, 91, 123; work hours of, 20, 31, 35, 44, 59, 61, 88, 91; working conditions of, 20, 38, 43–44, 49–50, 59–61, 84, 122–124. *See also* strikes

yellow fever epidemic, 24–26

Photo Acknowledgments

Library of Congress, pp. 2–3, 6, 26–27, 29, 33, 36, 39, 40, 42, 46, 55, 60, 65, 82, 90, 93, 127, 133; IPS, p. 8; United Mine Workers of America, pp. 11, 13, 56, 58, 61, 62, 72, 73, 94, 98 (bottom), 109 (bottom), 114, 115, 136; General Research Division, the New York Public Library, Astor, Lenox, and Tilden Foundations, p. 14; Brown Brothers, p. 17; Memphis/Shelby County Archives, Memphis/ Shelby County Public Library and Information Center, pp. 20, 24 (right); the Metropolitan Museum of Art, gift of Lyman C. Bloomingdale, 1901, p. 22; Tennessee State Library and Archives, p. 24 (left); the Western Reserve Historical Society, Cleveland, Ohio p. 34; North Carolina Division of Archives and History, p. 48; West Virginia State Archives, p. 52; Ohio Historical Society, p. 66; West Virginia and Regional History Collection, West Virginia University Libraries, pp. 70, 79, 89, 109 (top); Bettmann Archive, pp. 77, 86–87; Colorado Historical Society, pp. 97 (negative #F43381), 104 (negative #F33844), 111 (negative #F6692), 117 (negative #F9267), 118–119 (bottom; negative #F17.732); the Denver Public Library, Western History Department, pp. 98 (top), 118 (top); Illinois Labor History Society, pp. 103, 135, 137; Archives of Labor and Urban Affairs, Wayne State University, pp. 106, 112; Maurice Becker Papers, Archives of American Art, Smithsonian Institution, p. 121; Milwaukee County Historical Society, p. 123; Newberry Library, p. 126; Catholic University of America Archives, Terence Vincent Powderly Papers, p. 128.

Cover: portrait, Colorado Historical Society (negative #F33844); working children, IPS; author photo, Catherine Koemptgen.